knitting ARCHITECTURE

20 Patterns Exploring Form, Function, and Detail

Tanis Gray

INTERWEAVE.
interweave.com

EDITOR // Erica Smith with Kim Werker

TECHNICAL EDITOR // Kristen TenDyke

PHOTOGRAPHER // Joe Hancock

PHOTO STYLIST // Allie Liebgott

HAIR AND MAKEUP // Kathy MacKay

ASSOCIATE ART DIRECTOR // Julia Boyles

COVER & INTERIOR DESIGN // Adrian Newman

PRODUCTION // Kerry Jackson

Interweave
A division of F&W Media, Inc.
201 East Fourth Street
Loveland, CO 80537
interweave.com

Manufactured in China by RR Donnelley Shenzhen

Library of Congress Cataloging-in-Publication Data

Gray, Tanis.
  Knitting architecture : 20 patterns exploring form, function, and detail / Tanis Gray.
    pages cm
  Includes index.
  ISBN 978-1-59668-780-6 (pbk.)
  ISBN 978-1-59668-798-1 (PDF)
1. Knitting--Patterns. I. Title.
TT825.G66 2013
746.43'2--dc23

2013002145

10 9 8 7 6 5 4 3 2 1

ADDITIONAL PHOTOGRAPHY

Pages 9 and 13: (Cambridge College Chapel) © Dan Kite/iStockphoto. Pages 17 and 19: (Burj Al Arab) © Shao Weiwei/iStockphoto. Pages 21 and 27: (Sagrada Familia) © Rainer Walter Schmied/iStockphoto. Pages 29 and 33: (Porticus Octaviae) © Paolo Cipriani/iStockphoto. Page 35: (Sydney Architecture) © Steve Whitaker/iStockphoto. Page 40: (Sydney Opera House) © Fred Kamphues/Shutterstock. Page 43: (Wrought Iron Rosette) © Alan Tobey/ iStockphoto. Page 46: (Wrought Iron Circles) © Grigorios Moraitis/iStockphoto. Pages 49 and 50: (Fallingwater) © Robert Crow/Shutterstock. Pages 55 and 61: (Pompidou Center) © Jorge Felix Costa/Shutterstock. Pages 63 and 69: (1930's Home) © John Gollop/iStockphoto. Pages 71 and 76: (Tribute to Mucha) © Ellerslie/Shutterstock. Pages 79 and 85: (Municipal Building) © SeanPavonePhoto/Shutterstock. Pages 87 and 90: (Mosque at Manavgat) © Antony McAulay/Shutterstock. Pages 93 and 96: (Hagia Sophia) © wjarek/Shutterstock. Page 99: (Art Deco Swirls) © McKevin Shaughnessy/iStockphoto. Page 102: (Fisher Building) © Patricia Marks/Shutterstock. Pages 105 and 107: (Stanislas Square Lantern) © VII-photo/iStockphoto. Pages 113 and 118: (Leaning Tower of Pisa) © Jim Tardio Photography/iStockphoto. Page 121: (Bürogebäude) © areal17/iStockphoto. Page 125: (Bauhaus Building) © Claudio Divizia/Shutterstock. Pages 127 and 129: (Art Nouveau House) © Nikada/iStockphoto. Pages 133 and 136: (Bird's Nest) © AStock/Corbis. Pages 139 and 143: (Porch of the Caryatids) © Khirman Vladimir/Shutterstock.

contents

introduction

Have you ever stood in wonder, stopped dead in your tracks by a stunning building? How about by a beautiful sweater? We have dozens of museums the world over dedicated to architecture or apparel, but have you ever thought about how similar the two are?

I have always been fascinated by architecture. Something as simple as a large box in which we dwell can suddenly become a stunning, ultramodern structure, or be covered in ornate details inspired by movements in history, the climate, or a clever idea. Similarly, designing knitwear starts with an idea, a blueprint or schematic, math, materials, and a little bit of inspiration. A hat on the person in front of us at the grocery store, a flower on the side of a barren highway, a masterpiece hanging on the wall of a gallery, or a historic building in the middle of a modern city are all inspiration for what we can create with our knitting needles.

My husband, Roger, works at an engineering and architecture firm in Washington, D.C., as the director of sustainability. On our first date, we talked about our work—our passions and hobbies. I was struck by how incredibly different our paths and lines of work were, yet how similar the process was. The planning stages are the same (on much different scales), and the creative process and the taking and giving of ideas as we try to make the designs work can be difficult. In the end, we are both helping an idea come to life.

I hope this book inspires the designer and inner architect in all of us. Dream (and knit) to the limits of your imagination. That's what the designers in this book have done, and it is what makes our craft abundant with possibilities.

form FOLLOWS *function*

The simple idea that *"form follows function"*—first mentioned in 1852 by American sculptor Horatio Greenough and coined four decades later by American architect Louis Sullivan—would become a major factor in architectural plans and industrial design in the twentieth century. The idea is that the purpose of an object or building is of the utmost importance, and only after it is achieved then should design follow. Some modern architects have taken the idea of simple forms following function a step further and have chosen to have little or no ornamentation at all, believing that less is more.

This notion that a solid foundation, support structure, and a simple shell have utmost importance is easily applicable to the knitting world. Using our bodies as a foundation, we can create beautiful, effortless designs with elements borrowed from architecture. Like designers of buildings, designers of sweaters need to think critically about ornamentation and decide whether it enhances or hinders the end result.

The need for a strong, solid function is elemental. Similar to how structures need push and pull to help them move with the elements, we need our knitwear to be able to move with the push and pull of our bodies. Construction can be the difference between a garment and a garment with purpose. The gentle shaping of a neckline enforced by cables, ribbing on the side of a skirt to shape the form properly, or switching a stitch pattern at the waistline to accentuate its shape are all basic architectural choices we make before even casting on. Just like working on a building, we start by creating a blueprint based on a concept, and then we straighten out the basic construction, do the math, and begin.

king's college PULLOVER
Mari Muinonen

Evoking the vaults, buttresses, and ancient archways of Gothic buildings, this structured pullover by Mari Muinonen is wearable architecture. The nested cabling across the yoke under a ribbed collar creates the illusion of standing below the breathtaking ceilings of ancient buildings, staring up at them in wonder. These cables pull the yoke in to fit the bust and shoulders.

Finished measurements

About 31¼ (33½, 35, 37¼, 39½, 41¼, 42¾, 46½, 49¾, 51½, 54¼, 56¼, 58¾, 60¾)" (79.5 [85, 89, 94.5, 100.5, 105, 108.5, 118, 126.5, 131, 138, 143, 149, 154.5] cm) bust circumference.

Pullover shown measures 35" (89 cm) and is designed to be worn with slightly negative or no ease.

Yarn

DK weight (#3 light).

Shown here: Rowan Felted Tweed DK (50% merino wool, 25% alpaca, 25% viscose; 191 yd [175 m]/50 g): #175 cinnamon, 6 (6, 6, 7, 7, 7, 8, 8, 9, 9, 10, 10, 11, 11) skeins.

Needles

Size U.S. 5 (3.75 mm): 16", 24", and 32" (40, 60, and 80 cm) circular (cir) and set of 4 or 5 double-pointed (dpn).

Adjust needle sizes if necessary to obtain the correct gauge.

Notions

Markers (m); cable needle (cn); stitch holders or waste yarn; tapestry needle.

Gauge

21 sts and 27 rnds = 4" (10 cm) in St st, worked in rnds.

Notes: This pullover is worked seamlessly in the round from the top down.

Stitch Guide

SM1 Stitch Marker 1

SM2 Stitch Marker 2

Collar

Using shortest circular needle CO 112 (112, 112, 112, 112, 112, 126, 126, 126, 126, 126, 126, 126, 126) sts. Pm (SM1) for beg of rnd and join to work in the rnd, being careful not to twist sts.

EST RIB: (RS) *K1, p2, k2, p4, k2, p2, k1; rep from * around.

Work as est until piece meas 7½" (19 cm) from beg.

Yoke

PM FOR SHORT ROWS: Work Rnd 1 of Yoke Chart A for 6 reps, pm (SM2), then cont working Rnd 1 to end of rnd.

Work Rnd 2 of Yoke Chart A.

Shape Neck

Working in Yoke charts as indicated, shape neck with short rows as foll:

(*Note: The w&t sts for Rows 5–10 are indicated on the charts.*)

ROW 3: (RS) Work Row 3 of Yoke Chart A for 6 reps to SM2, w&t (see Techniques)—124 (124, 124, 124, 124, 124, 138, 138, 138, 138, 138, 138, 138, 138) sts.

ROW 4: (WS) Work Row 4 of Yoke Chart A for 6 reps to SM1, w&t.

ROW 5: Work Row 5 of Yoke Chart B for 1 rep, Yoke Chart A for 4 reps, then Yoke Chart C for 1 rep to 1 st before SM2, w&t.

ROW 6: Work Row 6 of Yoke Chart C for 1 rep, Yoke Chart A for 4 reps, then Yoke Chart B for 1 rep to 1 st before SM1, w&t.

ROW 7: Work Row 7 of Yoke Chart B for 1 rep, Yoke Chart A for 4 reps, then Yoke Chart C for 1 rep to 2 sts before SM2, w&t—135 (135, 135, 135, 135, 149, 149, 149, 149, 149, 149, 149, 149) sts.

ROW 8: Work Row 8 of Yoke Chart C for 1 rep, Yoke Chart A for 4 reps, then Yoke Chart B for 1 rep to 2 sts before SM1, w&t.

ROW 9: Work Row 9 of Yoke Chart B for 1 rep, Yoke Chart A for 4 reps, then Yoke Chart C for 1 rep to 4 sts before SM2, w&t.

ROW 10: Work Row 10 of Yoke Chart C for 1 rep, Yoke Chart A for 4 reps, then Yoke Chart B for 1 rep to 4 sts before SM1, w&t.

Shape Yoke

Cont working in the rnd as foll, and change to longer circs when sts no longer fit comfortably on shorter needle:

RND 11: (RS) Work Rnd 11 of Yoke Chart B for 1 rep, Yoke Chart A for 4 reps, Yoke Chart C for 1 rep, then Yoke Chart D for 2 (2, 2, 2, 2, 2, 3, 3, 3, 3, 3, 3, 3, 3) reps—150 (150, 150, 150, 150, 150, 166, 166, 166, 166, 166, 166, 166, 166) sts.

Cont working as est until Rnd 19 of all the charts is completed—192 (192, 192, 192, 192, 192, 216, 216, 216, 216, 216, 216, 216, 216) sts.

Cont working Yoke Chart A for all 8 (8, 8, 8, 8, 8, 9, 9, 9, 9, 9, 9, 9, 9) reps around, and pm between each chart rep on last rnd. Work Rnds 20–39 of Yoke Chart A—256 (256, 256, 256, 256, 256, 288, 288, 288, 288, 288, 288, 288) sts.

Sizes 33½ (35, 37¼, 39½, 41¼, 42¾, 46½, 49¾, 51½, 54¼, 56¼, 58¾, 60¾)" only:
Work 3 rnds of Yoke Chart A even.

INC RND: K1, M1 (see Techniques), work next rnd of Yoke Chart A to 1 st before m, M1, k1; rep from * around—16 (16, 16, 16, 16, 18, 18, 18, 18, 18, 18, 18, 18) sts inc'd.

Rep the last 4 rnds 0 (1, 2, 3, 4, 3, 4, 5, 6, 7, 8, 9, 10) more times—256 (272, 288, 304, 320, 342, 360, 369, 387, 405, 423, 441, 459) sts.

(*Note: For sizes 33½ (35, 37¼, 39½, 41¼, 42¾, 46½)": inc ends after Rnd 43 (47, 51, 55, 59, 55, 59) of chart. For sizes 49¾ (51½, 54¼, 56¼, 58¾, 60¾)": after Rnd 61 of chart, cont working in St st for all sts.*)

Sizes 31¼ (33½, 35, 37¼, 39½, 41¼)" only:
Divide for body and sleeves: (*Note: Change to shorter cir needle if sts do not comfortably fit on longer needle.*)

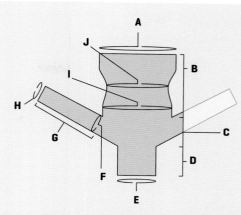

A - 32 [34¼, 35¾, 38, 40½, 42, 44½, 47¼, 50½, 52½, 55, 57, 59½, 61½]"
81.5 [87, 91, 96.5, 103, 106.5, 113, 120, 128.5, 133.5, 139.5, 145, 151, 156] cm

B - 17 [17½, 17½, 17½, 17½, 18, 18, 18, 18½, 18½, 18½, 19, 19, 19]"
43 [44.5, 44.5, 44.5, 44.5, 45.5, 45.5, 45.5, 47, 47, 47, 48.5, 48.5, 48.5] cm

C - 5 [5¼, 5¾, 6½, 7, 7½, 7, 7½, 8¼, 8¾, 9¼, 10, 10½, 11]"
12.5 [13.5, 14.5, 16.5, 18, 19, 18, 19, 21, 22, 23.5, 25.5, 26.5, 28] cm

D - 7½" 19 cm

E - 21¼ [21¼, 21¼, 21¼, 21¼, 21¼, 24, 24, 24, 24, 24, 24, 24, 24]"
54 [54, 54, 54, 54, 54, 61, 61, 61, 61, 61, 61, 61, 61] cm

F - 11¾ [12¼, 13, 13¼, 14½, 15¼, 15¼, 15½, 16¾, 17½, 18, 18¾, 19¾, 20½]"
30 [31, 33, 33.5, 37, 38.5, 38.5, 39.5, 42.5, 44.5, 45.5, 47.5, 50, 52] cm

G - 20½ [21, 21½, 21½, 21½, 21½, 22, 22, 22, 22, 22½, 22½, 22½, 22½]"
52 [53.5, 54.5, 54.5, 54.5, 54.5, 56, 56, 56, 56, 57, 57, 57, 57] cm

H - 10 [10, 10¾, 10¾, 10¾, 11½, 11½, 11½, 11½, 12¼, 12¼, 13, 13, 13]"
25.5 [25.5, 27.5, 27.5, 27.5, 29, 29, 29, 29, 31, 31, 33, 33, 33] cm

I - 31¼ [33½, 35, 37¼, 39½, 41¼, 42¾, 46½, 49¾, 51½, 54¼, 56¼, 58¾, 60¾]"
79.5 [85, 89, 94.5, 100.5, 105, 108.5, 118, 126.5, 131, 138, 143, 149, 154.5] cm

J - 27½ [29¾, 31¼, 33½, 35¾, 37¼, 40, 42¾, 46, 47¾, 50½, 52½, 55, 57]"
70 [75.5, 79.5, 85, 91, 94.5, 101.5, 108.5, 117, 121.5, 128.5, 133.5, 139.5, 145] cm

Work 6 (7, 7, 8, 8, 8) sts, place next 50 (50, 54, 56, 60, 64) sts onto st holder or waste yarn for left sleeve, use the backward loop method (see Techniques) to CO 6 (6, 6, 6, 7, 7) sts, pm for new beg of rnd, CO 6 (6, 6, 6, 7, 7) more sts, work 74 (78, 82, 88, 92, 96) sts for back, place next 50 (50, 54, 56, 60, 64) sts onto st holder or waste yarn for right sleeve, use the backward loop method to CO 6 (6, 6, 6, 7, 7) sts, pm side, CO 6 (6, 6, 6, 7, 7) more sts, work 74 (77, 81, 86, 91, 95) sts to end of rnd—172 (180, 188, 200, 212, 220) sts.

Sizes 42¾ (46½, 49¾, 51½, 54¼, 56¼, 58¾, 60¾)" only:

NEXT RND: Work as est to last 5 (4, 5, 5, 5, 5, 6, 6) sts.

Divide for body and sleeves: Place next 66 (68, 70, 74, 76, 80, 84, 88) sts onto st holder or waste yarn for left sleeve, use the backward loop method (see Techniques) to CO 6 (6, 8, 8, 8, 8, 9, 9) sts, pm for new beg of rnd, CO 6 (6, 8, 8, 8, 8, 9, 9) more sts, work 105 (112, 115, 120, 127, 132, 137, 142) sts for back, place next 66 (68, 70, 74, 76, 80, 84, 88) sts onto st holder or waste yarn for right sleeve, use the backward loop method to CO 6 (6, 8, 8, 8, 8, 9, 9) sts, pm for new beg of rnd, CO 6 (6, 8, 8, 8, 8, 9, 9) more sts, work 111 (118, 122, 127, 134, 139, 145, 150) sts to end of rnd—234 (248, 261, 271, 285, 295, 309, 319) sts.

Body

Sizes 31¼ (33½, 35, 37¼, 39½, 41¼, 42¾, 46½)" only:

Work body as foll and cont working Yoke Chart A until Rnd 61 is completed, then work all sts in St st.

For size 31¼" only: after working Rnd 41, there are 168 sts rem.

For all these sizes: after working Rnd 61, there are 164 (176, 184, 196, 208, 216, 230, 244) sts rem.

All sizes:

Work until piece meas 3" (7.5 cm) from divide.

Shape Waist

DEC RND: *K6, k2tog, knit to 8 sts before m, ssk (see Techniques), k6; rep from * once more—4 sts dec'd.

Work 5 rnds even.

Rep the last 6 rnds 4 more times—144 (156, 164, 176, 188, 196, 210, 224, 241, 251, 265, 275, 289, 299) sts rem.

Cont until piece meas 7½ (8, 8, 8, 8, 8½, 8½, 8½, 9, 9, 9, 9½, 9½, 9½)" (19 (20.5, 20.5, 20.5, 20.5, 21.5, 21.5, 21.5, 23, 23, 23, 24, 24, 24] cm) from divide.

INC RND: *K6, M1L (see Techniques), knit to 6 sts before m, M1R (see Techniques), k6; rep from * once more—4 sts inc'd.

Work 5 rnds even.

Rep the last 6 rnds 5 more times—168 (180, 188, 200, 212, 220, 234, 248, 265, 275, 289, 299, 313, 323) sts.

Cont until body measures 13 (13½, 13½, 13½, 13½, 14, 14, 14, 14½, 14½, 14½, 15, 15, 15)" (33 [34.5, 34.5, 34.5, 34.5, 35.5, 35.5, 35.5, 37, 37, 37, 38, 38, 38] cm) from divide.

Sizes 49¾ (54¼, 58¾)" only:

NEXT RND: Dec 1 st at beg of rnd—264 (288, 312) sts rem.

Sizes 42¾ (51½, 56¼, 60¾)" only:

NEXT RND: Inc 2 (1, 1, 1) sts evenly around—236 (276, 300, 324) sts.

All sizes:

EST RIB: *K2, p2; rep from * to end.

Work as est for 4" (10 cm). BO all sts.

Sleeve

Sizes 31¼ (33½, 35, 37¼, 39½, 41¼, 42¾, 46½)" only:

While working as instructed below, beg with Rnd 40 (44, 48, 52, 56, 60, 56, 60) of Yoke Chart A, work sleeve as foll and cont working chart until Rnd 61 is completed, then work all sts in St st.

Note: St counts will dec by 2 sts each after Rnds 40, 41, and 61.

All sizes:

Place 50 (50, 54, 56, 60, 64, 66, 68, 70, 74, 76, 80, 84, 88) held sts for 1 sleeve onto dpn. Beg at center of underarm CO sts, pick up and knit 7 (7, 7, 7, 8, 8, 7, 7, 9, 9, 9, 9, 10, 10) sts along first half of CO sts, work in patt to end, then pick up and knit 7 (7, 7, 7, 8, 8, 7, 7, 9, 9, 9, 9, 10, 10) sts along second half of CO sts—62 (64, 68, 70, 76, 80, 80, 82, 88, 92, 94, 98, 104, 108) sts.

Work 2 rnds even as est—60 (64, 68, 70, 76, 78, 80, 80, 88, 92, 94, 98, 104, 108) sts rem.

Shape Sleeve

DEC RND: K1, k2tog, work to last 3 sts, k2tog, k1—2 sts dec'd.

Work 7 (7, 7, 7, 5, 5, 5, 5, 3, 3, 3, 3, 3, 3) rnds even.

Rep the last 8 (8, 8, 8, 6, 6, 6, 6, 4, 4, 4, 4, 4, 4) rnds 2 (4, 4, 5, 8, 8, 8, 9, 13, 13, 14, 14, 17, 19) more times—52 (52, 56, 56, 56, 60, 60, 60, 60, 64, 64, 68, 68, 68) sts rem.

Work until sleeve measures 12 (12½, 13, 13, 13, 13, 13½, 13½, 13½, 13½, 14, 14, 14, 14)" (30.5 [31.5, 33, 33, 33, 33, 34.5, 34.5, 34.5, 35.5, 35.5, 35.5, 35.5] cm) from underarm.

EST RIB: *K2, p2; rep from * to end.

Cont as est for 8½" (21.5 cm). BO all sts.

Work second sleeve the same as the first.

Finishing

Weave in ends. Block to finished measurements.

Yoke Chart A

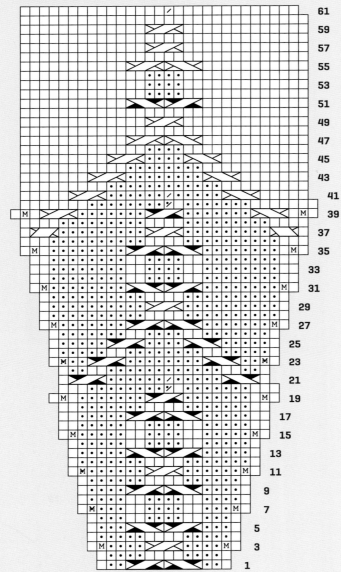

Yoke Chart B

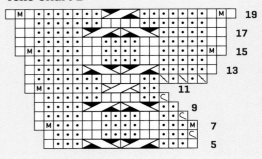

Yoke Chart C

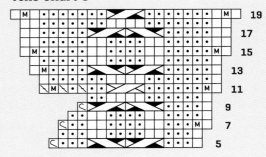

Yoke Chart D

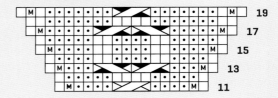

☐	knit on RS, purl on WS
⊡	purl on RS, knit on WS
Ⓜ	m1
◵	wrap and turn
◳	work wrap tog with wrapped st
◪	p2tog
◿	k2tog

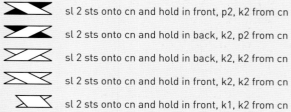

sl 2 sts onto cn and hold in front, p2, k2 from cn

sl 2 sts onto cn and hold in back, k2, p2 from cn

sl 2 sts onto cn and hold in back, k2, k2 from cn

sl 2 sts onto cn and hold in front, k2, k2 from cn

sl 2 sts onto cn and hold in front, k1, k2 from cn

sl 1 st onto cn and hold in back, k2, k1 from cn

burj al arab SKIRT
Olga Buraya-Kefelian

Olga Buraya-Kefelian has used yarn the same way an architect uses steel beams to lay out framework. In this case, simple dropped stitches against a background of stockinette, with a knitted-in waistband and applied I-cord hem, together create a very structured, flattering form. The skirt's airy and flowing dropped stitch side panels contrast against curved, finished shaping for a sense of playfulness found in the postmodern style.

Finished measurements
About 22¼ (26¼, 29¾, 33¾, 38½)" (56.5 [66.5, 75.5, 85.5, 98] cm) waist circumference.

Skirt shown measures 26¼" (66.5 cm) and is designed to be worn with little or no ease.

Yarn
Worsted weight (#4 medium).

Shown here: Louet MerLin Worsted (70% merino wool, 30% wet spun linen; 156 yd [143 m]/100 g): #43 pewter, 4 (5, 5, 6, 7) skeins.

Needles
Casing and Skirt: Size U.S. 7 (4.5 mm): two 24" (60 cm) circular (cir).

Applied I-Cord: Size U.S. 6 (4 mm): set of 4 or 5 double-pointed (dpn).

Adjust needle sizes if necessary to obtain the correct gauge.

Notions
Markers (m); waste yarn and size U.S. F/5 (3.75 mm) crochet hook; tapestry needle; 1" (2.5 cm) wide elastic, 1 yd (.9 m); sewing needle and matching thread.

Stitch Guide

Ladder Pattern

(multiple of 3 sts)

SET-UP RND: Yo, *k3, yo; rep from * to marker—inc'd to multiple of 4 sts + 1.

Knit as many rnds as indicated.

DROP RND: Drop next st from left needle and unravel it back to the yo made on the set-up rnd, *k3, drop next st from needle and unravel it back to the yo made on the set-up rnd; rep from * to m—dec'd to multiple of 3 sts.

Applied I-Cord

With WS facing and working yarn attached to live sts, use the cable or knitted method (see Techniques) to CO 3 sts onto left needle.

NEXT ROW: With RS facing and dpn, *k2, ssk, sl 3 sts from right needle to left needle; rep from * until all sts have been worked and only 3 sts rem on left needle.

NEXT ROW: S2kp (see Techniques)—1 st rem. Fasten off. Sew the 2 ends tog to join in the rnd.

Elastic Band

Prepare elastic band by measuring it around waist. Measure comfortably where you prefer skirt to rest. Cut elastic, then use sewing needle and matching thread to seam it closed. Set aside.

Casing

With waste yarn and crochet hook, use the provisional method (see Techniques) to CO 122 (144, 164, 186, 210) sts onto cir needle. Pm for beg of rnd and join to work in the rnd, being careful not to twist sts. Beg of rnd is at the left side seam of skirt.

With working yarn, knit 7 rnds.

TURNING RND: Purl.

Knit 6 rnds.

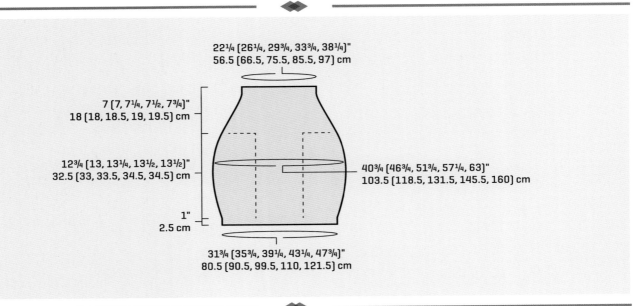

22¼ [26¼, 29¾, 33¾, 38¼]"
56.5 [66.5, 75.5, 85.5, 97] cm

7 [7, 7¼, 7½, 7¾]"
18 [18, 18.5, 19, 19.5] cm

12¾ [13, 13¼, 13½, 13½]"
32.5 [33, 33.5, 34.5, 34.5] cm

40¾ [46¾, 51¾, 57¼, 63]"
103.5 [118.5, 131.5, 145.5, 160] cm

1"
2.5 cm

31¾ [35¾, 39¼, 43¼, 47¾]"
80.5 [90.5, 99.5, 110, 121.5] cm

Join Casing

Carefully remove waste yarn from Provisional CO and place those sts on second cir needle. Fold work at turning rnd, insert elastic band inside casing, pinning in several places to keep it in place.

JOINING RND: Holding needles parallel with WS's together and elastic inside the casing, knit 1 st from each needle together all the way around.

Skirt

PM FOR SIDE SEAM: K61 (72, 82, 93, 105), pm for right side seam, knit to end.

Shape Hip

INC RND: *K1, M1, knit to 1 st before next m, M1, k1, sl m; rep from * once more—4 sts inc'd.

Knit 2 rnds even.

Rep the last 3 rnds 12 more times—174 (196, 216, 238, 262) sts.

Knit 0 (0, 2, 4, 6) rnds even. Piece meas about 7 (7, 7¼, 7½, 7¾)" (18 [18, 18.5, 19, 19.5] cm) to here.

PM FOR LADDER PATT: Remove beg of rnd m, k14 (18, 22, 24, 27), pm, k59 (62, 66, 71, 77), pm, k14 (18, 20, 24, 27), remove m, k25 (30, 32, 35, 39), pm, k37 (38, 42, 47, 53), pm for new beg of rnd. Beg of rnd is now toward the left front of skirt.

LADDER PATT SET-UP RND: *Work set-up rnd of Ladder patt (see Stitch Guide) to next m, sl m, knit to next m, sl m; rep from * once more—201 (229, 253, 279, 307) sts.

Cont working in St st until piece meas 12¾ (13, 13¼, 13½, 13½)" (32.5 [33, 33.5, 34.5, 34.5] cm) from Ladder patt set-up rnd.

LADDER PATT DROP RND: *Work drop rnd of Ladder patt to next m, sl m, knit to next m, sl m; rep from * once more—174 (196, 216, 238, 262) sts rem.

Knit 4 rnds even.

With dpn, work applied I-cord (see Stitch Guide) to BO sts.

Get Inspired

Burj Al Arab was built in 1999 in Dubai, inspired by the postmodern style, in which ornamentation and a sense of cleverness found its way back into design. It is a unique luxury hotel with an open atrium designed to mimic the shape of a ship's billowing sail.

Finishing

Weave in ends. Yarn used suggests machine wash on gentle cycle and dry in a dryer on Medium setting. Lay flat to finish. Press gently with warm iron.

sagrada familia CARDIGAN
Cirilia Rose

With dropped and wrapped stitches, bobbles, vertical and horizontal elements that accentuate the form by cinching in the waist, garter and stockinette stitch, Cirilia Rose's design dances on the line between the constructed Gothic period and ornate Art Nouveau style. With twisting columns of cables running vertically, this cardigan involves an array of techniques but never loses sight of putting function first.

Finished measurements

About 31.5 (37, 42½, 46¾, 51)" [80 (94, 108, 118.5, 129.5) cm] with 1¾" (4.5 cm) overlap for button band.

Cardigan shown measures 37" (94 cm) and is designed to be worn with little to no ease.

Yarn

Worsted weight (#4 medium).

Shown here: Imperial Stock Ranch Columbia (100% wool; 220 yd [201 m]/113 g): #114 dusty rose, 5 (6, 7, 7, 8) skeins.

Needles

Size U.S. 10 (6 mm): 32" (80 cm) circular (cir) and set of 4 or 5 double-pointed (dpn).

Adjust needle size if necessary to obtain the correct gauge.

Notions

Markers (m); stitch holders or waste yarn; cable needle (cn); tapestry needle; seven ½" (1.3 cm) buttons.

Gauge

14 sts and 20 rows = 4" (10 cm) in St st.

13 sts and 22 rows = 4" (10 cm) in Gtr st.

17 sts and 21 rows = 4" (10 cm) in Right and Left Twist patterns.

13½ sts and 20 rows = 4" (10 cm) in Open Column pattern.

Stitch Guide

Make Bobble (MB)

K1f&b (see Techniques) twice in same st, turn, p4, turn, ssk, k2tog, turn, p2tog.

Right Twist (RT)

K2tog leaving both sts on left needle, then knit first st again and sl both sts off left needle.

Left Twist (LT)

Skip first st, knit next st tbl, then knit first st and sl both sts off left needle.

Right Twist Pattern

(multiple of 4 sts)

ROW 1: (RS) *RT (see above), p2; rep from *.

ROW 2: *K2, p2; rep from *.

Rep Rows 1 and 2 for patt.

Left Twist Pattern

(multiple of 4 sts)

ROW 1: (RS) *LT (see above), p2; rep from *.

ROW 2: *K2, p2; rep from *.

Rep Rows 1 and 2 for patt.

Right Cable Panel

(panel of 4 sts)

ROWS 1, 3, AND 5: (RS) K4.

ROW 2 AND ALL WS ROWS: P4.

ROW 7: Sl 2 sts onto cn and hold in back, k2, k2 from cn.

ROW 8: P4.

Rep Rows 1–8 for patt.

Left Cable Panel

(panel of 4 sts)

ROWS 1, 3, AND 5: (RS) K4.

ROW 2 AND ALL WS ROWS: P4.

ROW 7: Sl 2 sts onto cn and hold in front, k2, k2 from cn.

ROW 8: P4.

Rep Rows 1–8 for patt.

Open Columns Pattern

(multiple of 8 sts + 2)

ROW 1: (RS) P2, *k1, k2tog, (yo) twice, ssk, k1, p2; rep from *.

ROW 2: K2, *p2, (p1, k1) into double yo, p2, k2; rep from *.

Rep Rows 1 and 2 for patt.

Garter Rib Pattern

(multiple of 6 sts + 1)

ROW 1: (WS) *K1, p2; rep from * to last st, k1.

ROW 2: (RS) P1, *k5, p1; rep from *.

Rep Rows 1 and 2 for patt.

Notes: Body is worked in one piece. Sleeves are knit in the round and joined with body before yoke decreases. Back neck is raised slightly with short rows.

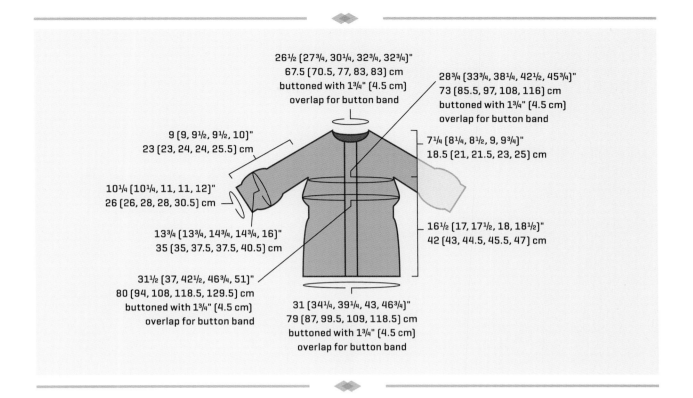

26½ [27¾, 30¼, 32¾, 32¾]"
67.5 [70.5, 77, 83, 83] cm
buttoned with 1¾" [4.5 cm]
overlap for button band

28¾ [33¾, 38¼, 42½, 45¾]"
73 [85.5, 97, 108, 116] cm
buttoned with 1¾" [4.5 cm]
overlap for button band

9 [9, 9½, 9½, 10]"
23 [23, 24, 24, 25.5] cm

7¼ [8¼, 8½, 9, 9¾]"
18.5 [21, 21.5, 23, 25] cm

10¼ [10¼, 11, 11, 12]"
26 [26, 28, 28, 30.5] cm

13¾ [13¾, 14¾, 14¾, 16]"
35 [35, 37.5, 37.5, 40.5] cm

16½ [17, 17½, 18, 18½]"
42 [43, 44.5, 45.5, 47] cm

31½ [37, 42½, 46¾, 51]"
80 [94, 108, 118.5, 129.5] cm
buttoned with 1¾" [4.5 cm]
overlap for button band

31 [34¼, 39¼, 43, 46¾]"
79 [87, 99.5, 109, 118.5] cm
buttoned with 1¾" [4.5 cm]
overlap for button band

Sleeve [make 2]

With dpn, CO 36 (36, 39, 39, 42) sts. Pm for beg of rnd and join to work in the rnd, being careful not to twist sts.

Purl 1 rnd, then knit 2 rnds.

BOBBLE RND: *K2, MB (see Stitch Guide); rep from * to end.

Knit 1 rnd.

INC RND: *K2, k1f&b; rep from * to end—48 (48, 52, 52, 56) sts.

Work in St st until piece meas 4 (4, 4½, 4½, 5)" (10 [10, 11.5, 11.5, 12.5] cm) from beg.

DEC RND: *K2, k2tog; rep from * to end—36 (36, 39, 39, 42) sts rem.

Work even in St st until piece meas 9 (9, 9½, 9½, 10)" (23 [23, 24, 24, 25.5] cm) from beg.

BO UNDERARM: BO 6 (6, 6, 6, 10) sts and knit to end of rnd—30 (30, 33, 33, 32) sts rem. Sl rem sts to st holder or waste yarn. Cut yarn and set aside.

Work second sleeve the same as the first.

Body

With cir needle, CO 128 (140, 160, 176, 192) sts. Do not join; work back and forth in rows.

Knit 4 rows.

EST PATT: (RS) Work 6 sts in Gtr st for buttonhole band, 2 sts in Rev St st, 28 (32, 36, 40, 44) sts in Right Twist patt, pm, 16 (16, 20, 24, 28) sts in Left Twist patt, pm, 4 sts in Right Cable Panel, 16 (20, 24, 24, 24) sts in Gtr st, 4 sts in Left Cable Panel, pm, 2 sts in Rev St st, 16 (16, 20, 24, 28) sts in Right Twist patt, pm, 28 (32, 36, 40, 44) sts in Left Twist patt, pm, 6 sts in Gtr st for button band.

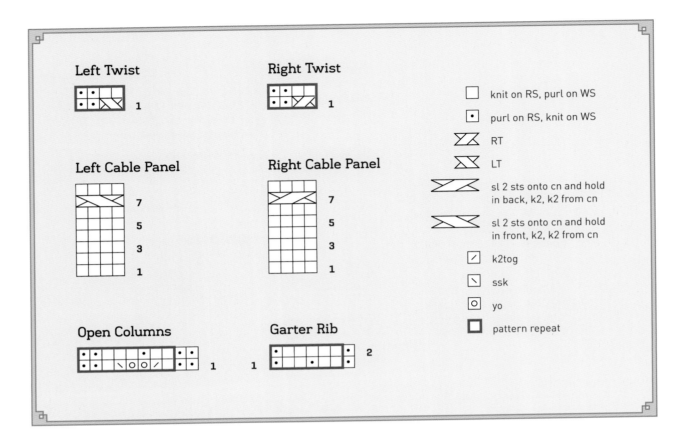

Left Twist 1

Right Twist 1

Left Cable Panel 7 5 3 1

Right Cable Panel 7 5 3 1

Open Columns 1 1

Garter Rib 2

☐ knit on RS, purl on WS

• purl on RS, knit on WS

RT

LT

sl 2 sts onto cn and hold in back, k2, k2 from cn

sl 2 sts onto cn and hold in front, k2, k2 from cn

k2tog

ssk

yo

pattern repeat

Cont as est until piece meas 10 (10, 11, 11½, 12)" (25.5 [25.5, 28, 29, 30.5] cm) from beg, ending with a WS row.

(Note: Read the following instructions before cont; buttonholes and patt are worked at the same time.)

BUTTONHOLE ROW: (RS) K3, yo, k2tog, work to end as est.

Work 9 (11, 11, 11, 11) rows even.

Rep the last 10 (12, 12, 12, 12) rows 5 more times, then rep Buttonhole Row once more. *At the same time,* when piece meas 10½ (11, 11½, 12, 12½)" (26.5 [28, 29, 30.5, 31.5] cm) from beg, end with a WS row.

EST PATT: (RS) Work 6 sts in Gtr st, work to next m in St st, remove m, work to next m in St st, sl m, work 4 sts in Right Cable Panel, 16 (20, 24, 24, 24) sts in St st, 4 sts in Left Cable Panel, sl m, work to next m in St st, remove m, work to last 6 sts in St st, work to end in Gtr st.

Cont as est until piece meas 12½ (13, 13½, 14, 14½)" (31.5 [33, 34.5, 35.5, 37] cm) from beg, ending with a RS (WS, WS, WS, WS) row.

Size 31.5" only:

DEC ROW: (WS) K6, p6, [p2tog, p8] 4 times, 4 sts in Left Cable Panel sts, 16 sts in Gtr st, 4 sts in Right Cable Panel, [p8, p2tog] 4 times, p6, k6—120 sts rem.

All sizes:

EST PATT: (RS) Work 6 sts in Gtr st, work 42 (50, 58, 66, 74) sts in Open Columns patt, sl m, work 4 sts in Right Cable Panel, 16 (20, 24, 24, 24) sts in Gtr st, 4 sts in Left Cable Panel, sl m, work 42 (50, 58, 66, 74) sts in Open Columns patt, 6 sts in Gtr st.

Cont as est until piece meas 15 (15½, 16, 16½, 17)" (38 [39.5, 40.5, 42, 43] cm) from beg, ending with a WS row.

Sizes 42½ [51]" only:

DEC ROW: (RS) K6, p2tog, [k1, k2tog, (yo) twice, ssk, k1 p2tog] 7 (9) times, work 4 sts in Right Cable Panel, k24, work 4 sts in Left Cable Panel, p2tog [k1, k2tog, (yo) twice, ssk, k1, p2tog] 7 (9) times, k6—144 (172) sts rem.

Sizes 31½ [37, 46¾]" only:

DEC ROW: (RS) K6, [p2tog, k1, k2tog, (yo) twice, ssk, k1] 3 (4, 5) times, p2, [k1, k2tog, (yo) twice, ssk, k1, p2tog] 2 (2, 3) times, work 4 sts in Right Cable Panel, k16 (20, 24), work 4 sts in Left Cable Panel, [p2tog, k1, k2tog, (yo) twice, ssk, k1] 2 (2, 3) times, p2, [k1, k2tog, (yo) twice, ssk, k1, p2tog] 3 (4, 5) times, k6—110 (128, 160) sts rem.

All sizes:

Cont as est, working p1 in place of p2 of Open Columns patt where dec'd, until piece meas 16½ (17, 17½, 18, 18½)" (42 [43, 44.5, 45.5, 47] cm) from beg, ending with a RS row.

DIVIDE FOR ARMHOLES: (WS) Work 25 (32, 35, 39, 40) sts as est for left front, BO 6 (6, 6, 6, 10) sts for underarm, work 48 (52, 62, 70, 72) sts as est for back, BO 6 (6, 6, 6, 10) sts for underarm, work to end as est for right front.

Yoke

JOINING ROW: (RS) Work as est across 25 (32, 35, 39, 40) right front sts, pm, return 30 (30, 33, 33, 32) held sleeve sts onto dpn and work across in St st, pm, work as est across 48 (52, 62, 70, 72) back sts, pm, return 30 (30, 33, 33, 32) held sleeve sts onto dpn and work across in St st, pm, work as est across 25 (32, 35, 39, 40) left front sts—158 (176, 198, 214, 216) sts.

Work 1 WS row even as est.

Shape Body

DEC ROW: (RS) *Work as est to 2 sts before first sleeve m, ssk, sl m, work to next sleeve m, sl m, k2tog; rep from * once more, then work to end as est—4 sts dec'd.

Work 3 (3, 1, 3, 3) rows even as est.

Rep the last 4 (4, 2, 4, 4) rows 1 (1, 4, 1, 2) more times—150 (168, 178, 206, 204) total sts rem; 23 (30, 30, 37, 37) sts each front, 30 (30, 33, 33, 32) sts each sleeve, 44 (48, 52, 66, 66) sts for back.

DEC ROW: (RS) K6, [p1, k1, k2tog, yo, ssk, k1] 2 (3, 3, 4, 4) times, p1, ssk, sl m, knit across sleeve to next m, sl m, k2tog, p1, [k1, k2tog, yo, ssk, k1, p1] 1 (1, 1, 2, 2) times, work 4 sts in Right Cable Panel, 16 (20, 24, 24, 24) sts in Gtr st, 4 sts in Left Cable Panel, [p1, k1, k2tog, yo, ssk, k1] 1 (1, 1, 2, 2) times, p1, ssk, sl m, knit across sleeve to next m, k2tog, p1, [k1, k2tog, yo, ssk, k1, p1] 2 (3, 3, 4, 4) times, k6—140 (156, 166, 190, 188) total sts rem; 20 (26, 26, 32, 32) sts each front, 30 (30, 33, 33, 32) sts each sleeve, 40 (44, 48, 60, 60) sts for back.

next sleeve m, sl m, p1, [ssk, k1, k2tog, p1] twice, k6—124 total sts rem; 15 sts each front, 30 sts each sleeve, 34 sts for back.

Work 1 WS row even as est.

BOBBLE ROW: (RS) K6, [p1, k1, MB, k1] twice, p1, sl m, knit to next sleeve m, p1, k1, MB, k1, p1, work 4 sts in Right Cable Panel, k16, work 4 sts in Left Cable Panel, p1, k1, MB, k1, p1, sl m, knit to next sleeve m, p1, [k1, MB, k1, p1] twice, k6.

Sizes 37 [42.5]" only:

DEC ROW: (RS) K6, [p1, ssk, k1, k2tog] 3 times, sl m, knit to next sleeve m, sl m, ssk, k1, k2tog, p1, work 4 sts in Right Cable Panel, k20 (24), work 4 sts in Left Cable panel, p1, ssk, k1, k2tog, sl m, knit to next sleeve m, sl m, [ssk, k1, k2tog, p1] 3 times, k6—132 (142) total sts rem; 18 sts each front, 30 (33) sts each sleeve, 36 (40) sts for back.

Work 1 WS row even as est.

BOBBLE ROW: (RS) K6, [p1, k1, MB, k1] 3 times, sl m, knit to next sleeve m, sl m, k1, MB, k1, p1, work 4 sts in Right Cable Panel, k20 (24), work 4 sts in Left Cable Panel, p1, k1, MB, k1, sl m, knit to next sleeve m, [k1, MB, k1, p1] 3 times, k6.

Sizes 46.75 [51]" only:

DEC ROW: (RS) K6, [p1, ssk, k1, k2tog] 3 times, p1, ssk, k2, sl m, knit to next sleeve m, sl m, k2, k2tog, p1, ssk, k1, k2tog, p1, work 4 sts in Right Cable Panel, k24, work 4 sts in Left Cable Panel, p1, ssk, k1, k2tog, p1, ssk, k2, sl m, knit to next sleeve m, sl m, k2, k2tog, p1, [ssk, k1, k2tog, p1] 3 times, k6—158 (156) total sts rem; 22 sts each front, 33 (32) sts each sleeve, 48 sts for back.

BOBBLE ROW: (RS) K6, [p1, k1, MB, k1] 4 times, sl m, knit to next sleeve m, sl m, [k1, MB, k1, p1] twice, work 4 sts in Right Cable Panel, k24, work 4 sts in Left Cable Panel, [p1, k1, MB, k1] twice, sl m, knit to next sleeve m, [k1, MB, k1, p1] 4 times, k6.

All sizes:

Work 1 WS row even as est, purling into st over each bobble.

DEC ROW: (RS) [Work as est to 1 st before bobble, s2kp] 2 (3, 3, 4, 4) times, work to sleeve m,

---

EST PATT: (WS) Work 6 sts in Gtr st, work to m in Garter Rib patt (aligning center Gtr st over the yo of the previous row), sl m, work in St st to next sleeve m, sl m, work in Garter Rib patt to cable panel m, sl m, work 4 sts in Right Cable Panel, work 16 (20, 24, 24, 24) sts in Gtr st, work 4 sts in Left Cable Panel, sl m, work to next sleeve m in Garter Rib patt, sl m, work in St st to next sleeve m, sl m, work in Garter Rib patt to last 6 sts, work Gtr st to end.

Work 2 (2, 2, 2, 2) more rows even as est, ending with a WS row.

Cont working as est; and shape body as foll:

DEC ROW: (RS) *Work as est to first sleeve m, sl m, k1, ssk, work to 3 sts before next sleeve m, k2tog, k1, sl m; rep from * once more, then work to end as est—4 sts dec'd.

Work 3 rows even as est.

Rep the last 4 rows 0 (1, 1, 2, 2) more times—136 (148, 158, 178, 176) total sts rem; 19 (24, 24, 29, 29) sts each front, 30 (30, 33, 33, 32) sts each sleeve, 38 (40, 44, 54, 54) sts for back.

Size 31.5" only:

DEC ROW: (RS) K6, [p1, ssk, k1, k2tog] twice, p1, sl m, knit to next sleeve m, sl m, p1, ssk, k1, k2tog, p1, work 4 sts in Right Cable Panel, k16, work 4 sts in Left Cable Panel, p1, ssk, k1, k2tog, p1, sl m, knit to remove m, [k1, k2tog] 10 (10, 11, 11, 10) times across sleeve, k0 (0, 0, 0, 2), remove m, [work as est to 1 st before bobble, s2kp] 2 (2, 2, 4, 4) times across back, work to sleeve m, remove m, k0 (0, 0, 0, 2), [k2tog, k1] 10 (10, 11, 11, 10) times across sleeve, remove m, [work as est to 1 st before bobble, s2kp] 2 (3, 3, 4, 4) times across front, work to end—100 (108, 116, 128, 128) total sts rem; 14 (17, 17, 20, 20) sts each front, 20 (20, 22, 22, 22) sts each sleeve, 32 (34, 38, 44, 44) sts for back.

Shape Yoke

Cont working all sts in Gtr st and shape yoke with short rows as foll:

Knit 9 rows, ending with a WS row.

SHORT ROWS 1 AND 2: Knit to last 34 sts, turn leaving rem sts unworked.

SHORT ROWS 3 AND 4: Knit to 4 sts before gap formed on previous row, turn leaving rem sts unworked.

Rep the last 2 short rows 3 more times, ending with a WS row.

NEXT ROW: (RS) Knit to end.

Work 5 rows in St st, ending with a WS row. BO all sts kwise.

Finishing

Sew underarm seam. Weave in ends and block to measurements. Sew on buttons opposite buttonholes.

Smocking

With yarn threaded on a tapestry needle, aligning with twist patterns, gently pinch fabric together in St st waistband as shown in photo (imagine the fabric as 2 uninterrupted columns). Wind yarn around these 2 pinched columns several times and fasten.

Get Inspired

Combining elements of Art Nouveau, Catalan modernism, and late Spanish Gothic architecture, the Sagrada Familia is an incomplete basilica in Barcelona. With sky-high spires on the exterior and hardly any flat surfaces in the interior, the nave is the centerpiece, filled with columns designed to allude to interlocking trees and abstract shapes in a spectrum of color.

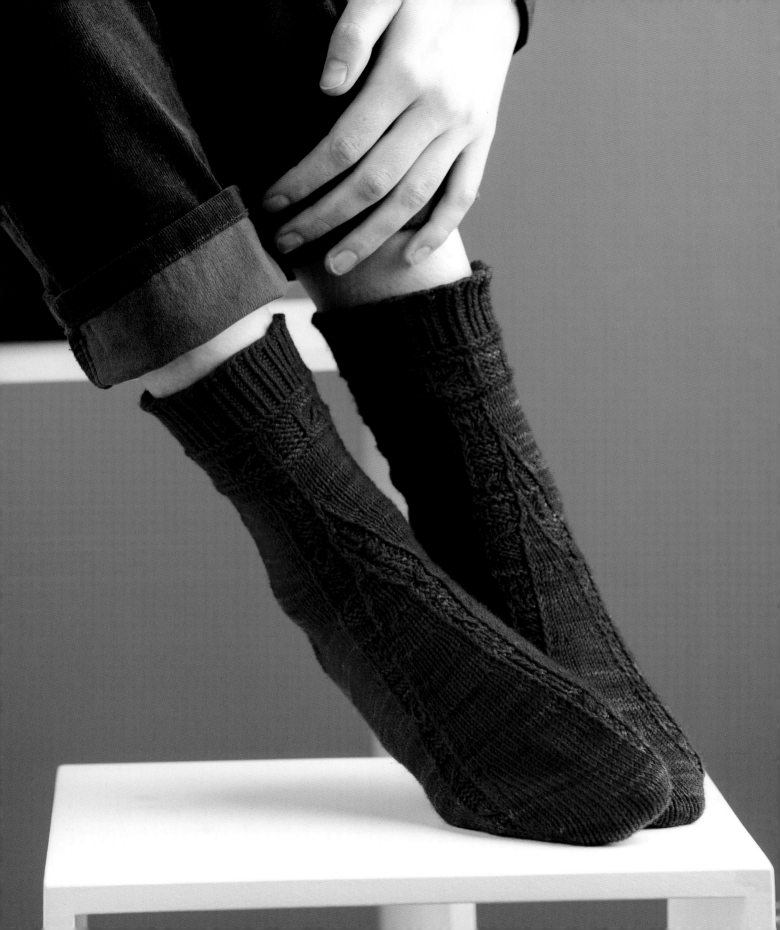

porticus SOCKS
Marjan Hammink

Marjan Hammink's socks, with their curved short-row heels creating form and geometric designs starting at the toe and working their way up the foot, are influenced by Romanesque architecture. This period, a precursor to the Gothic period, was known for its curved arches, simplistic layouts, massive structures, thick walls, towers, and columns.

Finished measurements

About 8 (8½)" (20.5 [21.5] cm) foot circumference.

About 9¼ (10)" (23.5 [25.5] cm) foot length.

Socks shown measure 8" (20.5 cm) circumference and are designed to be worn with no ease.

Yarn

Sock weight (#1 super fine).

Shown here: Wollmeise Sockenwolle 80/20 Twin (80% superwash merino wool, 20% polyamide; 510 yd [466 m]/150 g): Igor, 1 skein.

Needles

Size U.S. 1 (2.25 mm): set of 4 double-pointed (dpn).

Adjust needle size if necessary to obtain the correct gauge.

Notions

Markers (m); cable needle (cn); stitch holder or waste yarn; tapestry needle.

Gauge

30 sts and 46 rnds = 4" (10 cm) in St st worked in the rnd.

*(**Note:** Row gauge is important for proper fit of this project.)*

*****Notes:** The toe, instep, heel flap, and leg are patterned; the foot sole and heel turn are worked in stockinette stitch. The socks feature "gusset and flap" heels: work the gusset increases on the foot sole, turn the heel with short rows, and decrease the gusset stitches away as the heel flap is worked.*

Instep

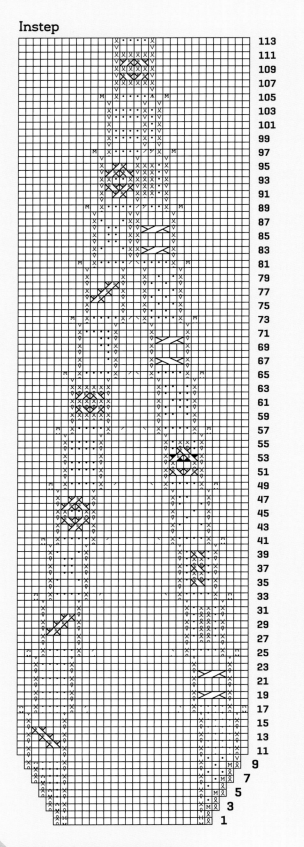

113
111
109
107
105
103
101
99
97
95
93
91
89
87
85
83
81
79
77
75
73
71
69
67
65
63
61
59
57
55
53
51
49
47
45
43
41
39
37
35
33
31
29
27
25
23
21
19
17
15
13
11
9
7
5
3
1

Heel

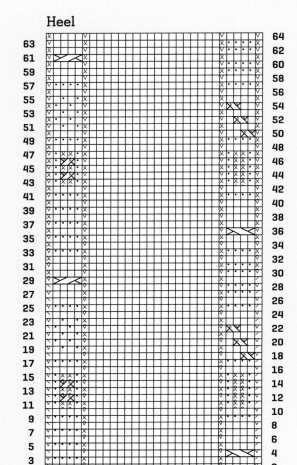

63   64
61   62
59   60
57   58
55   56
53   54
51   52
49   50
47   48
45   46
43   44
41   42
39   40
37   38
35   36
33   34
31   32
29   30
27   28
25   26
23   24
21   22
19   20
17   18
15   16
13   14
11   12
9   10
7   8
5   6
3   4
1   2

Toe

Using Judy's Magic Cast On (see Techniques), CO 24 sts—12 sts on each of 2 dpn. Divide sts over 3 dpn as foll: 12 sts on Needle 1 for instep and 6 sts each on Needles 2 and 3 for sole. Pm for beg of rnd and join to work in the rnd.

Knit 1 rnd.

INC RND: On Needle 1: k1, M1, knit to last st, M1, k1; on Needle 2: k1, M1, knit to end; on Needle 3: knit to last st, M1, k1—4 sts inc'd.

Rep the last 2 rows 3 more times—40 total sts; 20 sts on Needle 1, 10 sts each on Needles 2 and 3.

Knit 1 rnd.

EST PATT: On Needle 1: work Instep chart; on Needle 2: k1, M1, knit to end; on Needle 3: knit to last st, M1, k1—4 sts inc'd.

NEXT RND: On Needle 1: work Instep chart; on Needles 2 and 3: knit.

Rep the last 2 rnds 4 more times, ending after Rnd 10 of chart—60 total sts; 30 sts on Needle 1, 15 sts each on Needles 2 and 3.

Place 1 st from beg of Needle 2 onto Needle 1, and 1 st from end of Needle 3 onto Needle 1—32 sts on Needle 1, 14 sts each on Needles 2 and 3.

Size 8½" only:

Inc on Sole only as foll:

NEXT RND: On Needle 1: work Instep chart; on Needle 2: M1, knit to end; on Needle 3: knit to end, M1—2 sts inc'd.

NEXT RND: On Needle 1: work Instep chart; on Needles 2 and 3: knit.

Rep the last 2 rnds once more—64 sts total; 32 sts on Needle 1, 16 sts each on Needles 2 and 3.

Cuff

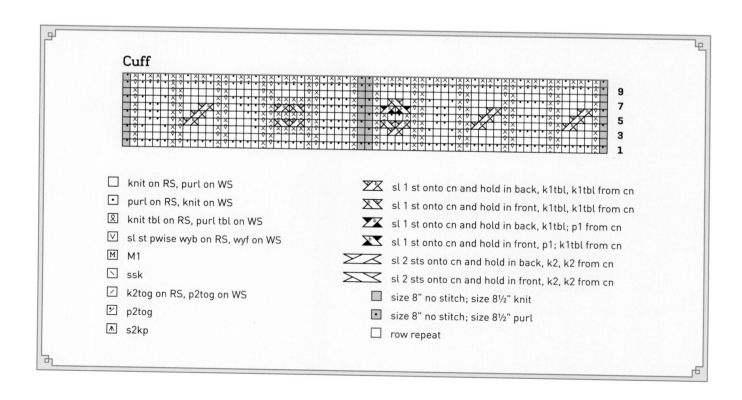

☐ knit on RS, purl on WS	sl 1 st onto cn and hold in back, k1tbl, k1tbl from cn
⊡ purl on RS, knit on WS	sl 1 st onto cn and hold in front, k1tbl, k1tbl from cn
⊠ knit tbl on RS, purl tbl on WS	sl 1 st onto cn and hold in back, k1tbl; p1 from cn
⊻ sl st pwise wyb on RS, wyf on WS	sl 1 st onto cn and hold in front, p1; k1tbl from cn
Ⓜ M1	sl 2 sts onto cn and hold in back, k2, k2 from cn
⊠ ssk	sl 2 sts onto cn and hold in front, k2, k2 from cn
⊿ k2tog on RS, p2tog on WS	☐ size 8" no stitch; size 8½" knit
⊡ p2tog	⊡ size 8" no stitch; size 8½" purl
⬚ s2kp	☐ row repeat

Foot

All sizes:

Cont working Instep chart on Needle 1 and St st on Needles 2 and 3 until piece meas 3¾ (4½)" (9.5 [11.5] cm) or 5½" (14 cm) less than total desired length from tip of toe.

Shape Gusset

INC RND: On Needle 1: work Instep chart; on Needle 2: knit to last 5 (7) sts, M1L, k5 (7); on Needle 3: k5 (7), M1R, knit to end—2 sts inc'd.

NEXT 2 RNDS: On Needle 1: work Instep chart; on Needles 2 and 3: knit.

Rep the last 3 rnds 13 more times—88 (92) total sts; 32 sts on Needle 1, 28 (30) sts each on Needles 2 and 3.

Heel Turn

ROW 1: (RS) On Needle 1: work Instep chart; on Needle 2: knit to last 5 (7) sts, M1L, k5 (7); on Needle 3: k5 (7), M1R, k8, w&t (see Techniques), leaving 14 sts unworked at end of Needle 3—90 (94) sts. Take note of the last row worked of Instep chart.

Sl sts on Needle 1 onto st holder or waste yarn and cont working back and forth on sole sts (Needles 2 and 3) only, working short rows as foll:

ROW 2: (WS) P28 (32), w&t leaving 14 sts unworked at end of Needle 2.

ROW 3: Knit to 1 st before wrapped st from previous row, w&t.

ROW 4: Purl to 1 st before wrapped st from previous row, w&t.

Rep the last 2 rows 8 more times, until 10 sts are wrapped on each Needle and 10 (14) sts rem unwrapped at center, ending with a WS row.

Return held sts back onto dpn and work in the rnd as foll:

NEXT RND: (RS) K5 (7) to end of Needle 2; on Needle 3: k15, pm for heel, knit to end working wraps together with the st they wrap (see Techniques) as they appear.

NEXT RND: On Needle 1: work Instep chart; on Needle 2: k14 (16), pm for heel, knit to last 5 (7) sts, working wraps together with the st they wrap as they appear, end here leaving rem sts unworked. Do not turn.

Size 8" only:

Sl 1 st from beg of Needle 1 to end of Needle 3, and 1 st from end of Needle 1 to beg of Needle 2—30 sts on Needle 1, 15 sts each on Needles 2 and 3.

Heel Flap

Sl 30 (32) sts from Needle 1 onto st holder or waste yarn. Cont working back and forth on 60 (62) sts for heel flap as foll:

SET-UP ROW: (RS) Knit to 6 sts before m, sl 1 pwise wyb, k4, ssk (1 st from each side of m), replace m, turn (do not wrap)—1 st dec'd.

ROW 1: (WS) Work Heel chart to m working last p2tog over 1 st from each side of m, replace m, turn (do not wrap)—1 st dec'd.

ROW 2: (RS) Work Heel chart to m working last ssk over 1 st from each side of m, replace m, turn (do not wrap)—1 st dec'd.

Rep the last 2 rows 12 more times, then work Row 1 once more, ending with WS Row 27 of chart—62 (66) total sts rem; 30 (32) sts on holder, 16 (17) sts each on Needles 2 and 3.

Return held sts back onto dpn and work in the rnd as foll:

DEC RND: (RS) Work Row 28 of Heel chart to m, working last ssk over 1 st from each side of m, replace m, k0 (1) to end of Needle 3—61 (65) sts rem.

DEC RND: On Needle 1: work 30 (32) sts in Instep chart; on Needles 2 and 3: k0 (1), work Row 29 of Heel chart to m working first k2tog over 1 st from each side of m and replacing m before the k2tog, sl m, k0 (1) to end of Needle 3—60 (64) total sts rem; 30 (32) sts on Needle 1, 15 (16) sts each on Needles 2 and 3.

EST PATT: On Needle 1: work 30 (32) sts in Instep chart; on Needles 2 and 3: k0 (1) to m, sl m, work Heel chart to next m, sl m, k0 (1) to end of Needle 3.

Cont working as est until Rnd 113 of Instep chart is completed.

Cuff

Work a horizontal herringbone as foll:

RND 1: Knit.

RND 2: *K2tog tbl but do not sl sts from needle, insert right needle between the 2 sts just knitted tog and knit the second st again, then sl both sts off the needle, sl the last st worked onto the left needle and rep from *.

RND 3: Knit.

Work Rnds 1–9 of Cuff chart.

Rep Rnds 1–3 of Horizontal Herringbone decreasing 0 (1) st on Rnd 3—60 (63) sts rem.

Ribbing

Work Rnd 10 of Cuff chart 11 (15) times.

Use Jeny's Surprisingly Stretchy BO (see Techniques) to BO all sts loosely.

Make a second sock to match the first.

Finishing

Weave in all ends. Block lightly.

Get Inspired

The Porticus Octaviae was built by Emperor Augustus for his sister, Octavia, in 27 B.C. in Rome. The structure was once home to three hundred columns, a quadriportico, or four-sided porch, and a library. With sections burned down and rebuilt many times, this structure collected a hodgepodge of different architectural styles over the centuries. Only a partial shell remains.

opera house SHELL
Suvi Simola

Suvi Simola's flattering pullover shell echoes Expressionist architecture, in which the structure is fragmented, distorted, or replicates naturally occurring geological elements. Cleverly placed short rows and waist shaping create a gentle, curving structure, and a unique curved bottom edge creates form by hugging the wearer's hips. A simple lace pattern adds a bit of intrigue and romance.

Finished measurements

About 34 (38, 42½, 46½, 50, 54)" (86.5 [96.5, 108, 118, 127, 137] cm) bust circumference.

Pullover shown measures 34" (86.5 cm) and is designed to be worn with slight positive ease.

Yarn

Worsted weight (#4 medium).

Shown here: Cascade Yarns Venezia Worsted (70% merino wool, 30% mulberry silk; 218 yd [200 m]/100 g): #160 ginger (MC), 3 (4, 4, 5, 5, 6) skeins; #108 autumn walk (CC), 1 skein.

Needles

Size U.S. 7 (4.5 mm): 16" and 32" (40 and 80 cm) circular (cir) and set of 2 double-pointed (dpn).

Adjust needle size if necessary to obtain the correct gauge.

Notions

Markers (m); stitch holder or waste yarn; tapestry needle.

Gauge

20 sts and 29 rnds/rows = 4" (10 cm) in St st worked in the rnd and in rows.

Stitch Guide

Lace Pattern
(multiple of 9 sts)

ROW 1: *K2tog, k2, yo, k1, yo, k2, ssk; rep from *.

ROWS 2 AND 4: Purl.

ROW 3: *K1, k2tog, yo, k3, yo, ssk, k1; rep from *.

ROW 5: Knit.

ROW 6: Purl.

Rep Rows 1–6 for patt.

Body

With CC and longer cir needle, CO 176 (196, 216, 236, 256, 276) sts. Pm for beg of rnd and join to work in the rnd, being careful not to twist sts.

Knit 1 rnd, purl 1 rnd.

NEXT RND: P44 (49, 54, 59, 64, 69), pm for center front, purl to end.

**Change to MC and shape the hem with short rows (worked around the center m) as foll:

SHORT ROW 1: (RS) Knit to 3 (3, 3, 4, 4, 4) sts before center m, w&t (see Techniques).

SHORT ROW 2: (WS) Purl to beg of rnd m, sl m, purl to 3 (3, 3, 4, 4, 4) sts before center m, w&t.

SHORT ROW 3: Knit to beg of rnd m, sl m, knit to 14 (16, 17, 19, 20, 22) sts before wrapped st of previous row, w&t.

SHORT ROW 4: Purl to beg of rnd m, sl m, purl to 14 (16, 17, 19, 20, 22) sts wrapped st of previous row, w&t.

Rep the last 2 short rows once more.

NEXT ROW: (RS) Knit to beg of rnd m.

NEXT RND: Knit, working the wraps together with the wrapped sts (see Techniques) as they appear.

NEXT RND: Change to CC and knit.

NEXT 2 RNDS: Purl.

Rep from ** 2 more times, removing the center m on the last rnd.

Cont with MC, working in St st as foll:

DEC RND: K2tog 1 (1, 0, 0, 1, 1) times, k86 (96, 108, 118, 126, 136), pm to indicate side "seam," k2tog 1 (1, 0, 0, 1, 1) times, knit to end—174 (194, 216, 236, 254, 274) sts rem.

Shape Waist

DEC RND: *K1, k2tog, knit to 3 sts before m, ssk, k1, sl m; rep from * once more—4 sts dec'd.

Work 5 (5, 7, 7, 7, 9) rnds even.

Rep the last 6 (6, 8, 8, 8, 10) rnds 2 (5, 1, 3, 5, 1) more times—162 (170, 208, 220, 230, 266) sts rem.

Sizes 34 (42½, 46½, 54)" only:

[Rep dec rnd, then work 3 (5, 5, 7) rnds even] 3 (4, 2, 4) times—150 (192, 212, 250) sts rem.

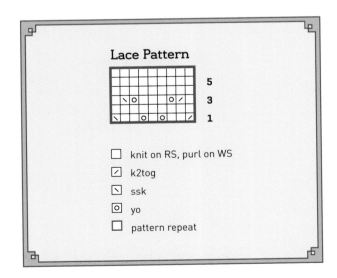

Lace Pattern

□ knit on RS, purl on WS
☑ k2tog
☒ ssk
⊙ yo
□ pattern repeat

All sizes:

Work 4 (2, 2, 2, 0, 0) rnds even.

INC RND: *K1, M1L, knit to 1 st before m, M1R, k1, sl m; rep from * once more—4 sts inc'd.

Work 3 rnds even.

Rep the last 4 rnds once more—158 (178, 200, 220, 238, 258) sts.

[Rep inc rnd, then work 5 rnds even] 3 times—170 (190, 212, 232, 250, 270) sts.

Work even in St st until piece meas 14 (14½, 15, 15½, 16, 16½)" (35.5 [37, 38, 39.5, 40.5, 42] cm) from beg, measured from lowest part of the hem.

Divide for Armholes

NEXT RND: *Knit to 5 (6, 6, 7, 7, 8) sts before m, BO next 10 (12, 12, 14, 14, 16) sts removing the m; rep from * once more—75 (83, 94, 102, 111, 119) sts rem for each front and back. Cont working back and forth in St st on front sts only. Sl back sts to st holder or waste yarn.

Front

Knit 1 RS row.

Shape Armholes

BO 3 (4, 4, 5, 4, 6) sts at the beg of next 2 rows, then BO 1 (2, 3, 4, 4, 4) st(s) at the beg of foll 2 rows—67 (71, 80, 84, 95, 99) sts rem.

Sizes 42½ (46½, 50, 54)" only:

BO 2 (2, 3, 3) sts at the beg of next 2 rows—76 (80, 89, 93) sts rem.

Sizes 50 (54)" only:

BO 2 sts at the beg of next 2 rows—85 (89) sts rem.

All sizes:

PURL RIDGE: Knit 1 WS row, purl 1 RS row.

Purl 1 WS row.

EST LACE PATT: Work 2 (4, 2, 4, 2, 4) sts in St st, pm, work 63 (63, 72, 72, 81, 81) sts in Lace patt, pm, work 2 (4, 2, 4, 2, 4) sts in St st.

Cont working as est until armholes meas 7¾ (8¼, 8¾, 9¼, 9¾, 10¼)" (19.5 [21, 22, 23.5, 25, 26] cm), ending with a WS row.

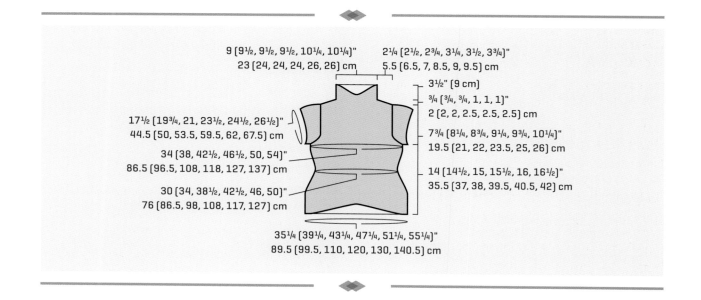

9 (9½, 9½, 9½, 10¼, 10¼)"
23 (24, 24, 24, 26, 26) cm

2¼ (2½, 2¾, 3¼, 3½, 3¾)"
5.5 (6.5, 7, 8.5, 9, 9.5) cm

3½" (9 cm)

¾ (¾, ¾, 1, 1, 1)"
2 (2, 2, 2.5, 2.5, 2.5) cm

17½ (19¾, 21, 23½, 24½, 26½)"
44.5 (50, 53.5, 59.5, 62, 67.5) cm

7¾ (8¼, 8¾, 9¼, 9¾, 10¼)"
19.5 (21, 22, 23.5, 25, 26) cm

34 (38, 42½, 46½, 50, 54)"
86.5 (96.5, 108, 118, 127, 137) cm

14 (14½, 15, 15½, 16, 16½)"
35.5 (37, 38, 39.5, 40.5, 42) cm

30 (34, 38½, 42½, 46, 50)"
76 (86.5, 98, 108, 117, 127) cm

35¼ (39¼, 43¼, 47¼, 51¼, 55¼)"
89.5 (99.5, 110, 120, 130, 140.5) cm

Shape Shoulders

Cont working in St st and work short rows as foll:

SHORT ROWS 1 AND 2: Work to last 4 (4, 5, 4, 5, 5) sts, w&t.

SHORT ROWS 3 AND 4: Work to last 8 (8, 10, 8, 9, 10) sts, w&t.

SHORT ROWS 5 AND 6: Work to last 11 (12, 14, 12, 13, 15) sts, w&t.

Sizes 46½ (50, 54)" only:

SHORT ROWS 7 AND 8: Work to last 16 (17, 19) sts, w&t.

All sizes:

Work 2 rows, knitting or purling the wraps together with the wrapped sts as they appear.

Place sts onto a st holder or waste yarn, cut yarn leaving a tail about 12" (30.5 cm) long, and set aside.

Back

Return 75 (83, 94, 102, 111, 119) held back sts to longer cir needle and join MC preparing to work a RS row.

Work same as for front, keeping sts on needle after shoulder shaping.

Join Shoulders

Sl 11 (12, 14, 16, 17, 19) sts from right back onto dpn, then sl 11 (12, 14, 16, 17, 19) sts from right front onto a second dpn. With yarn tail threaded on tapestry needle join these sts using the Kitchener st (see Techniques). Rep for left shoulder—45 (47, 48, 48, 51, 51) sts rem for neck on each front and back.

Collar

Sl 45 (47, 48, 48, 51, 51) held front sts onto shorter cir needle, then sl 45 (47, 48, 48, 51, 51) back sts onto shorter cir needle, pm for beg of rnd.

NEXT RND: *[K2tog] 1 (1, 0, 0, 1, 1) times, k43 (45, 48, 48, 49, 49); rep from * once more—88 (92, 96, 96, 100, 100) sts rem.

NEXT RND: K22 (23, 24, 24, 25, 25), pm for center front, knit to end.

Change to CC.

Knit 1 rnd and purl 2 rnds.

***Change to MC and shape the collar with short rows (worked around the center m) as foll:

SHORT ROW 1: (RS) Knit to 3 (3, 3, 4, 4, 4) sts before center m, w&t.

SHORT ROW 2: (WS) Purl to beg of rnd m, sl m, purl to 3 (3, 3, 4, 4, 4) sts before center m, w&t.

SHORT ROW 3: Knit to beg of rnd m, sl m, knit to 7 sts before wrapped st of previous row, w&t.

SHORT ROW 4: Purl to beg of rnd m, sl m, purl to 7 sts before wrapped st of previous row, w&t.

Rep the last 2 short rows once more.

NEXT ROW: Knit to beg of rnd m.

NEXT RND: Knit, working the wraps together with the wrapped sts as they appear.

NEXT RND: Change to CC and knit.

NEXT 2 RNDS: Purl with CC.

Rep from *** once more, removing the center m on the last rnd.

Knit 1 more rnd with CC, then BO all sts.

Sleeve

With shorter cir needle, MC and RS facing, beg at center of underarm BO sts, pick up and knit 9 (12, 15, 18, 20, 23) sts along armhole BO sts, then pick up and knit 69 (75, 75, 81, 83, 86) sts evenly around the armhole to the BO sts on the other side, pick up and knit 9 (12, 15, 18, 20, 23) sts along rem BO sts—87

(99, 105, 117, 123, 132) sts. Pm for beg of rnd and join for working in the rnd.

Change to CC and pm for cap shaping as follows:

NEXT RND: *K29 (33, 35, 39, 41, 44), pm; rep from * once more, then knit to end.

Purl 2 rnds.

Shape Cap

**Change to MC and shape cap with short rows as foll:

SHORT ROW 1: (RS) Knit to second m, sl m, k15 (18, 18, 21, 21, 21), w&t.

SHORT ROW 2: (WS) Purl to second marker, sl m, p15 (18, 18, 21, 21, 21), w&t.

SHORT ROW 3: Knit to second marker, sl m, k10 (12, 12, 14, 14, 14), w&t.

Get Inspired

The Sydney Opera House, completed in 1973, is an Expressionist structure influenced by elements of Gothic, Romanesque, and Rococo architecture. Curved elements are given depth and texture by the Swedish tiles that cover the exterior.

SHORT ROW 4: Purl to second marker, sl m, p10 (12, 12, 14, 14, 14), w&t.

SHORT ROW 5: Knit to second marker, sl m, k5 (6, 6, 7, 7, 7), w&t.

SHORT ROW 6: Purl to second marker, sl m, p5 (6, 6, 7, 7, 7), w&t.

NEXT ROW: Knit to beg of rnd m, working wraps together with the wrapped sts as they appear.

NEXT RND: Knit, working the wraps together with the wrapped sts as they appear.

NEXT RND: Change to CC and knit.

NEXT 2 RNDS: Purl with CC.

Rep from ** once more, removing the 2 cap shaping m on the last rnd.

Knit 1 more rnd with CC, then BO all sts.

Rep for second sleeve.

Finishing

Weave in ends. Block to measurements.

wrought iron TOTE
Angela Hahn

Angela Hahn's sturdy, textured, and reinforced Fair Isle tote bag is a nod to Paris's decorative wrought iron work seen on gates, doors, fences, and grilles from the Art Deco period. Beginning in Paris in the 1920s, Art Deco took the world by storm, borrowing motifs from the Aztec, African, and Egyptian cultures and using materials such as crystal, stainless steel, Bakelite, and inlay.

Finished measurements
12" (31 cm) wide × 6" (15 cm) deep × 8½" (21.5 cm) tall (excluding strap).

Yarn
Worsted weight (#4 medium).

Shown here: Brooklyn Tweed Shelter (100% targhee-columbia wool; 140 yd [128 m]/50 g): #23 fossil (MC), 2 skeins; #16 pumpernickel (CC) 2 skeins.

Needles
Base and Straps: Size U.S. 6 (4 mm): 24" (60 cm) circular (cir) and double-pointed (dpn).

Body: Size U.S. 7 (4.5 mm): 24" (60 cm) cir.

Adjust needle sizes if necessary to obtain the correct gauge.

Notions
Markers (m); stitch holder or waste yarn; tapestry needle; heavy canvas or other lining fabric, 1 yd (0.9 m); interfacing or plastic needlepoint canvas; paper (for lining pattern); sewing needle; matching heavy sewing thread.

Gauges
20 sts and 30 rnds = 4" (10 cm) in St st with smaller needle, worked in rnds.

21 sts and 24 rnds = 4" (10 cm) in Fair Isle with larger needle, worked in rnds.

Notes: To help hide jog when yarn color changes at the beg of a rnd, try slipping the first st of the next rnd.

Base

With CC and smaller cir needle, CO 192 sts. Pm for beg of rnd and join to work in the rnd, being careful not to twist sts.

PM AS FOLL: K64, pm, k32, pm, k64, pm, k32.

DEC RND: *K2tog, [k5, k2tog] 8 times, k4, ssk, sl m, k2tog, [k4, k2tog] 4 times, k4, ssk, sl m; rep from * once more—160 total sts rem; 54 sts each long edge, 26 sts each short edge.

Shape Base

RND 1: Knit.

RND 2: *K2tog, knit to 2 sts before next m, ssk; rep from * 3 more times—8 sts dec'd.

Rep the last 2 rnds 11 more times, changing to dpn when sts no longer fit comfortably on cir needle—64 total sts rem; 30 sts each long edge, 2 sts each short edge.

JOIN CENTER: Place the st just knit, 30 sts from adjacent long edge, and 1 st from opposite short edge onto 1 dpn, and the rem 32 sts onto a second dpn. Turn work inside out (purl side is facing out) and use the three-needle BO (see Techniques) to join sts together.

Body

Beg at any corner of Base, with WS facing and CC, use smaller cir to pick up and knit 1 st for each CO st—192 total sts; 64 sts each long side, 32 sts each short side. Break yarn. Turn work so RS is facing. Join CC at right-hand corner of a long edge and pm for beg of rnd.

SET-UP RND: K64, pm, k32, pm, k64, pm, k32. Each m should be at a corner of the base.

Change to MC and knit 8 rnds.

Work Rnd 1 of Parigi pattern chart.

Change to larger needles and work Rnds 2–37 of Parigi chart.

Change to smaller needles and work Rnd 38 of Parigi chart.

With MC only, knit 8 rnds.

DIVIDE FOR STRAPS: *K16, BO 32 sts, k16, remove m, k16, M1 (see Techniques), k16, remove m; rep from * once more, k16 to edge of BO sts—65 sts rem on each side. Cont working back and forth on one strap and sl 65 sts for the other strap to st holder or waste yarn.

Parigi Pattern

37
35
33
31
29
27
25
23
21
19
17
15
13
11
9
7
5
3
1

□ with MC knit

◆ with CC knit

□ pattern repeat

First introduced at the Exposition Internationale des Arts Décoratifs et Industriels Modernes (International Exposition of Modern Industrial and Decorative Arts), Art Deco differed greatly from its predecessor, Art Nouveau. Art Deco was more angular and symmetrical, influenced by styles such as cubism, futurism, and modernism. Seen in everything from jewelry to railway stations, this style was particularly embraced by post–World War I America and Europe.

Strap
Shape Strap

Dec every other row as foll:

ROW 1: (WS) P1, k2tog, knit to last 3 sts, k2tog, p1—2 sts dec'd.

ROW 2: (RS) K1, *sl 1 pwise wyb, k1; rep from * to end.

ROW 3: Rep Row 1—2 sts dec'd.

ROW 4: K2, *sl 1 pwise wyb, k1; rep from * to last st, k1.

Rep the last 4 rows 10 more times—21 sts rem.

Dec every 4th row as foll:

ROW 1: (WS) P1, knit to last st, p1.

ROW 2: (RS) K2, *sl 1 pwise wyb, k1; rep from * to last st, k1.

ROW 3: P1, k2tog, k to last 3 sts, k2tog, p1—2 sts dec'd.

ROW 4: K1, *sl 1 pwise wyb, k1; rep from * to end.

ROW 5: Rep Row 1.

ROW 6: Rep Row 4.

ROW 7: Rep Row 3—2 sts dec'd.

ROW 8: Rep Row 2.

Rep Rows 1–4 once more—15 sts rem.

ROW 1: (WS) P1, knit to last st, p1.

ROW 2: K1, *sl 1 pwise wyb, k1; rep from * to end.

Rep the last 2 rows until piece meas 12" (30.5 cm) from divide. Break yarn and place sts on st holder or waste yarn.

Return 65 held sts from other side of body to smaller cir and join MC preparing to work a WS row. Work second strap the same as the first, but do not break yarn. Place sts for each strap on two dpn and use three-needle BO to join together.

Finishing

Weave in loose ends and block to measurements. If desired, cut piece of plastic needlepoint canvas to fit base, and sew into place with sewing needle and heavy thread. Use bag (including strap) as template to make paper pattern for lining. Base of finished lining should be about ¼" (6 mm) smaller than base of bag; top of finished lining should fall about ¼" (6 mm) to ½" (1.3 cm) below top of bag, and finished lining for strap should be ½" (1.3 cm) to ¾" (2 cm) narrower than strap. Use paper pattern to cut lining pieces as foll: It is recommended to place seams at each corner and at sides of base to reinforce rectangular shape. If desired, use interfacing to stiffen lining. Insert lining into bag and use sewing needle and heavy thread to slip-stitch top and strap edges of lining into place.

fallingwater HAT
Katharina Nopp

Katharina Nopp's clever hat creates a snug form for the wearer's head. The twisted ribbing and eye-catching texture of the alternating stockinette and reverse stockinette sections create plateaus in multiple directions, much like the structures of the Prairie School style of architecture. Spinning off of the Arts and Crafts movement, the Prairie School designers wished to start a new era of architecture that was distinctly American.

Finished measurements

15¾ (17½, 19¼)" (40 [44.5, 49] cm) circumference; stretches to fit 19¾ (21½, 23¼)" (50 [54.5, 59] cm) head circumference.

Yarn

DK weight (#3 light).

Shown here: Dream in Color Everlasting DK (100% superwash merino wool, 275 yd [251 m]/100 g): Carolina, 1 skein.

Needles

Size U.S. 6 (4 mm): 16" (40 cm) circular (cir) and set of 4 double-pointed (dpn).

Adjust needle size if necessary to obtain the correct gauge.

Notions

Marker (m); tapestry needle.

Gauge

23 sts and 30 rnds = 4" (10 cm) in St st, worked in rnds.

Note: Body of hat is worked in the round to the top of the crown, where sts are divided over 4 dpns. The sts on two of the dpns (across from each other) are grafted together, then the sts on the rem 2 needles are knit for additional rows before being grafted together.

Brim

With cir needle, CO 90 (100, 110) sts. Pm for beg of rnd and join to work in the rnd, being careful not to twist sts.

EST RIBBING: *P1, k1tbl; rep from *.

Cont as est for 12 (14, 14) more rnds.

Body

RNDS 1–8: [P1, k1tbl] 6 (7, 7) times, p1, knit to end.

RND 9: [P1, k1tbl] 6 (7, 7) times, p1, k12, p10, knit to last 22 sts, pm, k12, p10.

RNDS 10–13: [P1, k1tbl] 6 (7, 7) times, p1, k12, p10, knit to m, sl m, k12, p10.

RNDS 14–18: [P1, k1tbl] 6 (7, 7) times, p17, knit to end.

RNDS 19–23: [P1, k1tbl] 6 (7, 7) times, p1, knit to m, sl m, p10, knit to end.

RNDS 24–28: [P1, k1bl] 6 (7, 7) times, p1, k8, p14, knit to m, sl m, k6, purl to end.

RNDS 29–33: [P1, k1tbl] 6 (7, 7) times, p13, knit to end.

RNDS 34–38: [P1, k1tbl] 6 (7, 7) times, p1, knit to m, sl m, p14, knit to end.

RNDS 39–43: [P1, k1tbl] 6 (7, 7) times, p17, knit to m, sl m, k10, purl to end.

RND 44: [P1, k1tbl] 6 (7, 7) times, knit to end.

Rep the last rnd 14 (17, 20) more times, ending last rnd 3 (4, 5) sts before end of rnd.

Break yarn.

Finishing

Divide sts over 4 dpn as follows: sl next 19 (23, 25) sts onto Needle 1, 26 (27, 30) sts onto Needle 2, 19 (23, 25) sts onto Needle 3, and 26 (27, 30) sts onto Needle 4.

Cont working on Needle 3 only as foll:

Join yarn preparing to work a RS row and work 10 (12, 14) rows in St st, ending with a WS row. Break yarn.

Get Inspired

The most recognized example of the Prairie School of architecture is Frank Lloyd Wright's Fallingwater, with its overhanging eaves, long horizontal planes, flat roofs, and complete integration into the surrounding landscape.

With about 12" (30.5 cm) of yarn threaded on tapestry needle, join sts on Needles 2 and 4 using the Kitchener st (See Techniques). Rep for sts on Needles 1 and 3.

Weave in ends. Block to measurements.

the
details

Ornamentation is more than just the icing on the cake of a structure. Often ornamentation provides a purpose, whether it's reinforcing the interior, supporting a roof, or helping with water drainage. Other times it's less structural but nonetheless an important factor in the look and feel of a building—its overall personality.

Specifically with regard to knitting, details bear the touches of interest that inspire people to admire and recreate. The pieces in this chapter are modeled after structures that boast a high level of detail and capture the imagination, from the majestic lines of the Chrysler Building against the New York City skyline, to the off-the-wall ornamentation of the Pompidou Center in Paris.

The details of lace, texture, ruffles, ruching, colorwork, and other embellishments make for interesting knitting and become even more interesting conversation. You will see that the designers have created something not only pleasing to the eye, but also utilitarian.

pompidou WRAP
Grace Anna Farrow

Knitted as individual triangles then joined as you go, Grace Anna Farrow's striped wrap boasts a construction that is as clever as the style of architecture it is based on—a hybrid of high-tech and postmodern styles. The building that inspires it features its inside and outside on view at the same time, and this is echoed in the garment by using fingering-weight yarn in highly contrasting colors that render each stitch visible. The increases and decreases create sharp zigzags that serve as the wrap's support structure.

Finished measurements
27" (68.5 cm) wide × 65" (165 cm) long.

Yarn
Fingering weight (#1 super fine).

Shown here: Isager Alpaca 1 (100% baby alpaca; 437 yd [400 m]/50 g): #30 black (A), 3 skeins.

Fingering weight (#1 super fine).

Shown here: Isager Alpaca 2 (50% baby alpaca, 50% merino lambswool; 270 yd (247 m)/50 g): #8s medium natural brown (B), #21 red (C), #23 green gray (D), #7s light natural brown (E): 1 skein each.

Needles
Size U.S. 6 (4 mm): straight and 40" (100 cm) circular (cir).

Adjust needle size if necessary to obtain the correct gauge.

Notions
Markers (m); stitch holders or waste yarn; tapestry needle.

Gauge
20 sts and 32 rows = 4" (10 cm) in St st, lightly blocked.

Notes: Circular needles are used to accommodate large number of sts. Do not join; work back and forth in rows.

Foundation Triangles [make 5]

With straight needles and A, CO 1 st.

ROW 1: (RS) [K1, yo, k1] into st—3 sts.

ROWS 2 AND 4: Purl.

ROW 3: K1, M1, pm, k1, M1, k1—5 sts.

INC ROW: (RS) K1, M1, knit to m, M1, sl m, k1, M1, knit to last st, M1, k1—4 sts inc'd.

NEXT ROW: Purl.

Rep the last 2 rows 10 more times—49 sts.

Break yarn and place sts and m onto st holder or waste yarn. Make 4 more the same as the first, leaving the sts on the needle and keeping yarn attached to the last triangle.

Section 1

Change to cir needle and cont working with B as foll:

ROW 1: (RS) Ssk, knit to m, M1, sl m, k1, M1, knit to last st, M1, k1—51 sts.

ROW 2: Knit.

Break yarn B.

Cont working with A as foll:

ROW 1: (RS) Ssk, knit to m, M1, sl m, k1, M1, knit to last st, M1, k1—2 sts inc'd.

ROW 2: Purl.

Rep the last 2 rows 11 more times—75 sts.

Section 2

Keeping A attached, cont working with C as foll:

ROW 1: (RS) Ssk, knit to m, M1, sl m, k1, M1, knit to last st, sl last st to right needle, sl 49 held sts from a foundation triangle onto left needle preparing to work a RS row, return the last slipped st from the right needle to the left needle, pm, then knit the last st together with the first 2 sts of foundation triangle, using s2kp (see Techniques) knit to m, M1, sl m, k1, M1, knit to last st, M1, k1—126 sts.

ROW 2: Knit.

Break yarn C.

Cont working with A as foll:

ROW 1: Ssk, knit to m, M1, sl m, k1, M1, knit to 1 st before next m, sl 1 st, remove m, return slipped st to left needle, replace m, s2kp , knit to next m, M1, sl m, k1, M1, knit to last st, M1, k1—2 sts inc'd.

ROW 2: Purl.

Rep the last 2 rows 11 more times—150 sts.

Section 3

Keeping A attached, cont with D as foll:

ROW 1: (RS) Ssk, knit to m, M1, sl m, k1, M1, knit to 1 st before next m, sl 1 st, remove m, return slipped st to left needle, replace m, s2kp, knit to next m, M1, sl m, k1, M1, knit to last st, sl last st to right needle, sl 49 held sts from a foundation triangle onto left needle preparing to work a RS row, return the last slipped st from the right needle to the left needle, pm, then knit the last st together with the first 2 sts of foundation triangle using s2kp, knit to m, M1, sl m, k1, M1, knit to last st, M1, k1—201 sts.

ROW 2: Knit.

Break yarn D.

Cont working with A as foll:

ROW 1: Ssk, *knit to next m, M1, sl m, k1, M1, knit to 1 st before next m, sl 1 st, remove m, return slipped st to left needle, replace m, s2kp ; rep from * once more, knit to next m, M1, sl m, k1, M1, knit to last st, M1, k1—2 sts inc'd.

ROW 2: Purl.

Rep the last 2 rows 11 more times—225 sts.

Section 4

Keeping A attached, cont with E as foll:

ROW 1: (RS) Ssk, *knit to next m, M1, sl m, k1, M1, knit to 1 st before next m, sl 1 st, remove m, return slipped st to left needle, replace m, s2kp; rep from * once more, knit to next m, M1, sl m, k1, M1, knit to last st, sl last st to right needle, sl 49 held sts from a foundation triangle onto left needle preparing to work a RS row, return the last slipped st from the right needle to the left needle, pm, then knit the last st together with the first 2 sts of foundation triangle using s2kp, knit to m, M1, sl m, k1, M1, knit to last st, M1, k1—276 sts.

ROW 2: Knit.

Break yarn E.

Cont working with A as foll:

ROW 1: Ssk, *knit to next m, M1, sl m, k1, M1, knit to 1 st before next m, sl 1 st remove m, return slipped st to left needle, replace m, s2kp ; rep from * 2 more times, knit to next m, M1, sl m, k1, M1, knit to last st, M1, k1—2 sts inc'd.

ROW 2: Purl.

Rep the last 2 rows 11 more times—300 sts.

work a RS row, return the last slipped st from the right needle to the left needle, pm, then knit the last st together with the first 2 sts of foundation triangle using s2kp, knit to m, M1, sl m, k1, M1, knit to last st, M1, k1—351 sts.

ROW 2: Knit.

Break yarn B.

Cont working with A as foll:

ROW 1: (RS) Ssk, *knit to next m, M1, sl m, k1, M1, knit to 1 st before next m, sl 1 st remove m, return slipped st to left needle, replace m, s2kp ; rep from * 3 more times, knit to next m, M1, sl m, k1, M1, knit to last st, M1, k1—2 sts inc'd.

ROW 2: Purl.

Rep the last 2 rows 11 more times—375 total sts; 24 sts in each narrow section and 51 sts in each wide section.

Section 6

Keeping A attached, cont with C as foll:

ROW 1: (RS) Ssk, *knit to next m, M1, sl m, k1, M1, knit to 1 st before next m, sl 1 st, remove m, return slipped st to left needle, replace m, s2kp; rep from * 3 more times, knit to m, M1, sl m, k1, M1, knit to last 2 sts, k2tog.

ROW 2: Knit.

Break yarn C.

Cont working with A as foll:

ROW 1: (RS) Ssk, *knit to next m, M1, sl m, k1, M1, knit to 1 st before next m, sl 1 st, remove m, return slipped st to left needle, replace m, s2kp; rep from * 3 more times, knit to next m, M1, sl m, k1, M1, knit to last 2 sts, k2tog.

ROW 2: Purl.

Rep the last 2 rows 11 more times.

Section 5

Keeping A attached, cont with B as foll:

ROW 1: (RS) Ssk, *knit to next m, M1, sl m, k1, M1, knit to 1 st before next m, sl 1 st, remove m, return slipped st to left needle, replace m, s2kp; rep from * 2 more times, knit to next m, M1, sl m, k1, M1, knit to last st, sl last st to right needle, sl 49 held sts from a foundation triangle onto left needle preparing to

Section 7

Keeping A attached, cont with D as foll:

ROW 1: (RS) Ssk, *knit to next m, M1, sl m, k1, M1, knit to 1 st before next m, sl 1 st, remove m, return slipped st to left needle, replace m, s2kp; rep from * 3 more times, knit to next m, M1, sl m, k1, M1, knit to last 2 sts, k2tog.

ROW 2: Knit.

Break yarn D.

With A, cont working sts before first m only as foll:

ROW 1: (RS) Ssk, knit to 1 st before next m, sl 1 st, remove m, return slipped st to left needle, k2tog, turn—23 sts rem; 350 sts rem on needle to be worked later.

ROW 2: Purl.

ROW 3: Ssk, knit to last 2 sts, k2tog—2 sts dec'd.

ROW 4: Purl.

Rep the last 2 rows 9 more times—3 sts rem.

NEXT ROW: (RS) S2kp—1 st rem. Break A and pull tail through last st to fasten off.

Join A and cont working rem 350 sts on needle as foll:

ROW 1: (RS) Ssk, *knit to 1 st before next m, sl 1 st, remove m, return slipped st to left needle, replace m, s2kp, knit to next m, M1, sl m, k1, M1; rep from * 3 more times, knit to last 2 sts, k2tog—2 sts dec'd.

ROW 2: Purl.

Rep the last 2 rows 11 more times—326 sts rem.

Section 8

Keeping A attached, cont with E as foll:

ROW 1: (RS) Ssk, *knit to 1 st before next m, sl 1 st, remove m, return slipped st to left needle, replace m, s2kp, knit to next m, M1, sl m, k1, M1; rep from * 3 more times, knit to last 2 sts, k2tog—324 sts rem.

ROW 2: Knit.

Break yarn E.

With A, cont working sts before second m only as foll:

ROW 1: (RS) Ssk, knit to 1 st before next m, sl 1 st, remove m, return slipped st to left needle, replace m, s2kp, knit to 1 st before next m, sl 1 st, remove m, return slipped st to left needle, k2tog, turn—45 sts rem; 275 sts rem on needle to be worked later.

ROW 2: Purl.

ROW 3: Ssk, knit to next m, sl 1 st, remove m, return slipped st to left needle, replace m, s2kp, knit to last 2 sts, k2tog—4 sts dec'd.

ROW 4: Purl.

Rep the last 2 rows 10 more times—5 sts rem.

NEXT ROW: (RS) Sl 3, k2tog, pass 3 slipped sts over k2tog—1 st rem. Break A and pull tail through last st to fasten off.

Join A and cont working rem 275 sts on needle as foll:

ROW 1: (RS) Ssk, *knit to 1 st before next m, sl 1 st, remove m, return slipped st to left needle, replace m, s2kp, knit to next m, M1, sl m, k1, M1; rep from * 2 more times, knit to last 2 sts, k2tog—2 sts dec'd.

ROW 2: Purl.

Rep the last 2 rows 11 more times—251 sts rem.

Section 9

Keeping A attached, cont with B as foll:

ROW 1: (RS) Ssk, *knit to 1 st before next m, sl 1 st, remove m, return slipped st to left needle, replace m, s2kp, knit to next m, M1, sl m, k1, M1; rep from * 2 more times, knit to last 2 sts, k2tog—249 sts rem.

ROW 2: Knit.

Break yarn B.

With A, cont working sts before second m only as foll:

ROW 1: (RS) Ssk, knit to 1 st before next m, sl 1 st, remove m, return slipped st to left needle, replace m, s2kp, knit to 1 st before next m, sl 1 st, remove m, return slipped st to left needle, k2tog, turn—45 sts rem; 200 sts rem on needle to be worked later.

ROW 2: Purl.

m, s2kp, knit to next m, M1, sl m, k1, M1; rep from * once more, knit to last 2 sts, k2tog—2 sts dec'd.

ROW 2: Purl.

Rep the last 2 rows 11 more times—176 sts rem.

Section 10

Keeping A attached, cont with C as foll:

ROW 1: (RS) Ssk, *knit to 1 st before next m, sl 1 st, remove m, return slipped st to left needle, replace m, s2kp, knit to next m, M1, k1, M1; rep from * 3 more times, knit to last 2 sts, k2tog—174 sts rem.

ROW 2: Knit.

Break yarn C.

With A, cont working sts before second m only as foll:

ROW 1: (RS) Ssk, knit to 1 st before next m, sl 1 st, remove m, return slipped st to left needle, replace m, s2kp, knit to 1 st before next m, sl 1 st, remove m, return slipped st to left needle, k2tog, turn—45 sts rem; 125 sts rem on needle to be worked later.

ROW 2: Purl.

ROW 3: Ssk, knit to next m, sl 1 st, remove m, return slipped st to left needle, replace m, s2kp, knit to last 2 sts, k2tog—4 sts dec'd.

ROW 4: Purl.

Rep the last 2 rows 10 more times—5 sts rem.

NEXT ROW: (RS) Sl 3, k2tog, pass 3 slipped sts over k2tog—1 st rem. Break A and pull tail through last st to fasten off.

Join A and cont working rem 125 sts on needle as foll:

ROW 1: (RS) Ssk, knit to 1 st before next m, sl 1 st, remove m, return slipped st to left needle, replace m, s2kp, knit to next m, M1, sl m, k1, M1, knit to last 2 sts, k2tog—2 sts dec'd.

ROW 2: Purl.

Rep the last 2 rows 11 more times—101 sts rem.

ROW 3: Ssk, knit to next m, sl 1 st, remove m, return slipped st to left needle, replace m, s2kp, knit to last 2 sts, k2tog—4 sts dec'd.

ROW 4: Purl.

Rep the last 2 rows 10 more times—5 sts rem.

NEXT ROW: (RS) Sl 3, k2tog, pass 3 slipped sts over k2tog—1 st rem. Break A and pull tail through last st to fasten off.

Join A and cont working rem 200 sts on needle as foll:

ROW 1: (RS) Ssk, *knit to 1 st before next m, sl 1 st, remove m, return slipped st to left needle, replace

Section 11

Keeping A attached, cont with D as foll:

ROW 1: (RS) Ssk, knit to 1 st before next m, sl 1 st, remove m, return slipped st to left needle, replace m, s2kp, knit to next m, M1, sl m, k1, m, knit to last 2 sts, k2tog—99 sts rem.

ROW 2: Knit.

Break yarn D.

With A, cont working sts before second m only as foll:

ROW 1: (RS) Ssk, knit to 1 st before next m, sl 1 st, remove m, return slipped st to left needle, replace m, s2kp, knit to 1 st before next m, sl 1 st, remove m, return slipped st to left needle, k2tog, turn—45 sts rem; 50 sts rem on needle to be worked later.

ROW 2: Purl.

ROW 3: Ssk, knit to next m, sl 1 st, remove m, return slipped st to left needle, replace m, s2kp, knit to last 2 sts, k2tog—4 sts dec'd.

ROW 4: Purl.

Rep the last 2 rows 10 more times—5 sts rem.

NEXT ROW: (RS) Sl 3, k2tog, pass 3 slipped sts over k2tog—1 st rem. Break A and pull tail through last st to fasten off.

Join A and cont working rem 50 sts on needle as foll:

ROW 1: (RS) Ssk, knit to last 2 sts, k2tog—2 sts dec'd.

ROW 2: Purl.

Rep the last 2 rows 11 more times—26 sts rem.

Section 12

Keeping A attached, cont with E as foll:

ROW 1: (RS) Ssk, knit to last 2 sts, k2tog—24 sts rem.

ROW 2: Knit.

Break yarn E.

With A, cont working as foll:

ROW 1: (RS) Ssk, knit to last 2 sts, k2tog—2 sts dec'd.

ROW 2: Purl.

Rep the last 2 rows 11 more times—2 sts rem.

NEXT ROW: K2tog—1 st rem. Break A and pull tail through last st to fasten off.

Finishing

Lightly block piece to be rectangular. Weave in all ends.

Get Inspired

Paris's Pompidou Center, an example of high-tech architecture, is located in the 4th arrondissement. It is not unlike looking at an X-ray: you can see both the exterior frame and the brightly colored tubes making up the interior HVAC system. Housing Europe's largest modern art museum, a library, and an acoustic research facility, this seemingly skeletal building is a modern beacon in an old city.

arts and crafts CARDIGAN
Amy Christoffers

Worked from the bottom up to the armhole shaping, Amy Christoffers's reverse stockinette stitch and cabled lace cardigan is an ode to the Arts and Crafts movement. The fresh, elegant design evokes what designers of that movement desired in its clean lines, strong structures, organic design elements, and a functional fold-over ribbed collar. The classic combination of wool with leather buttons brings to mind the natural elements that these designers were so fond of incorporating into their finished objects.

Finished measurements

About 32¾ (36, 39¼, 42½, 45½, 48¾)" (83 [91.5, 99.5, 108, 115.5, 124] cm) bust circumference, buttoned with 1¼" (3.2 cm) overlapped button band.

Cardigan shown measures 36" (91.5 cm) and is designed to be worn with slight ease.

Yarn

Worsted weight (#4 medium).

Shown here: Peace Fleece Worsted (70% wool, 30% mohair; 200 yd [183 m]/113 g): Lauren's Coral, 5 (5, 6, 6, 7, 7) skeins.

Needles

Ribbing: Size U.S. 8 (5 mm): 24" (60 cm) circular (cir) and set of 4 or 5 double-pointed (dpn).

Body and Sleeves: Size U.S. 9 (5.5 mm): 24" (60 cm) cir and set of 4 or 5 dpn.

Adjust needle sizes if necessary to obtain the correct gauge.

Notions

Markers (m); cable needle (cn); stitch holders or waste yarn; tapestry needle; five 1" (2.5 cm) buttons.

Gauge

15 sts and 22 rows = 4" (10 cm) in Rev St st with larger needles; 13 sts = 2¾" (7 cm) in Arts and Crafts Panel with larger needles.

Stitch Guide

K1, p1 Rib

Flat

(multiple of 2 sts + 1)

ROW 1: (WS) P1, *k1, p1; rep from *.

ROW 2: (RS) K1, *p1, k1; rep from *.

Rep Rows 1 and 2 for patt.

Circular

(multiple of 2 sts)

RND 1: *K1, p1; rep from *.

Rep Rnd 1 for patt.

Arts and Crafts Panel

(panel of 13 sts—also, see chart)

Flat

ROW 1: (RS) P1, k1, p1, sl 2 sts onto cn and hold in back, k1, k2 from cn, k1, sl 1 st onto cn and hold in front, k2, k1 from cn, p1, k1, p1.

ROWS 2 AND 4: (WS) K1, p1, k1, p7, k1, p1, k1.

ROW 3: K2tog, yo, p1, k1, k2tog, yo, k1, yo, ssk, k1, p1, yo, ssk.

ROW 5: P1, k1, p1, k2tog, yo, k3, yo, ssk, p1, k1, p1.

ROW 6: Rep Row 2.

Rep Rows 1–6 for patt.

Circular

RND 1: (RS) P1, k1, p1, sl 2 sts onto cn and hold in back, k1, k2 from cn, k1, sl 1 st onto cn and hold in front, k2, k1 from cn, p1, k1, p1.

RNDS 2 AND 4: P1, k1, p1, k7, p1, k1, p1.

RND 3: K2tog, yo, p1, k1, k2tog, yo, k1, yo, ssk, k1, p1, yo, ssk.

RND 5: P1, k1, p1, k2tog, yo, k3, yo, ssk, p1, k1, p1.

RND 6: Rep Rnd 2.

Rep Rnds 1–6 for patt.

Arts and Crafts Chart

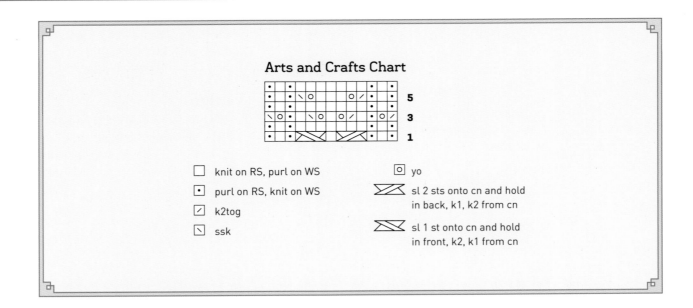

knit on RS, purl on WS

• purl on RS, knit on WS

k2tog

ssk

o yo

sl 2 sts onto cn and hold in back, k1, k2 from cn

sl 1 st onto cn and hold in front, k2, k1 from cn

Body

With smaller cir, CO 129 (141, 153, 165, 177, 189) sts. Do not join; work back and forth in rows.

Work k1, p1 rib (see Stitch Guide) until piece meas 3" (7.5 cm) from beg, ending with a WS row. Change to larger cir.

EST PATT: (RS) Work 12 (12, 12, 14, 14, 14) sts in Rev St st, work 13 sts in Arts and Crafts Panel (see Stitch Guide), work 8 (11, 14, 15, 18, 21) sts in Rev St st, pm for side, work 7 (10, 13, 14, 17, 20) sts in Rev St st, work 13 sts in Arts and Crafts Panel, work 23 (23, 23, 27, 27, 27) sts in Rev St st, 13 sts in Arts and Crafts Panel, 7 (10, 13, 14, 17, 20) sts in Rev St st, pm for side, work 8 (11, 14, 15, 18, 21) sts in Rev St st, work 13 sts in Arts and Crafts Panel, work 12 (12, 12, 14, 14, 14) sts in Rev St st.

Cont working even as est until piece meas 5" (12.5 cm) from beg, ending with a RS row.

Shape Waist

DEC ROW: (WS) Work as est to 3 sts before m, ssk, k1, sl m, k2tog, work as est to 2 sts before next m, ssk, sl m, k1, k2tog, work to end— 4 sts dec'd.

Work 11 rows even, ending with a RS row.

Rep dec row—121 (133, 145, 157, 169, 181) sts rem.

Work 17 rows even, ending with a RS row.

INC ROW: (WS) Work to 1 st before m, M1, k1, sl m, M1, work to next m, M1, sl m, k1, M1, work to end— 4 sts inc'd.

Work 11 rows even, ending with a RS row.

Rep inc row—129 (141 153, 165, 177, 189) sts.

Cont working even as est until piece meas 17" (43 cm) from beg, ending with a WS row.

DIVIDE FRONTS AND BACK: (RS) Work right front to 4 (5, 5, 6, 7, 7) sts before m, BO the next 7 (9, 9, 11, 13, 13) sts, work back to 3 (4, 4, 5, 6, 6) sts before next m, BO the next 7 (9, 9, 11, 13, 13) sts, work left front to end—29 (31, 34, 36, 38, 41) sts rem each front and 57 (61, 67, 71, 75, 81) sts rem for back. Cont working back and forth on sts for left front. Sl sts for back and right front onto st holders or waste yarn.

Left Front
Shape Neck and Armhole

DEC ROW 1: (WS) K1, ssk, work to end as est—28 (30, 33, 35, 37, 40) sts rem.

DEC ROW 2: (RS) P1, p2tog, work to last 3 sts, ssp, p1—2 sts dec'd.

NEXT ROW: Work even as est.

Rep the last 2 rows 2 (3, 4, 4, 5, 6) more times—22 (22, 23, 25, 25, 26) sts rem.

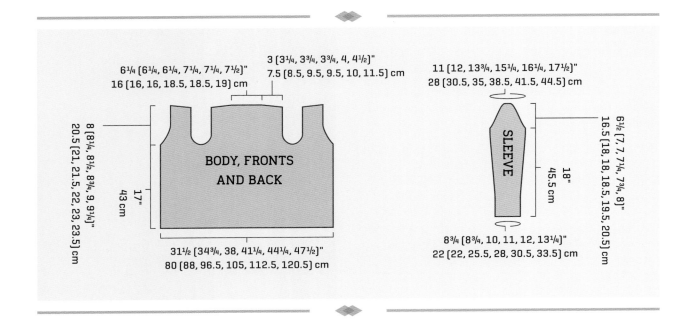

6¼ [6¼, 6¼, 7¼, 7¼, 7½]"
16 [16, 16, 18.5, 18.5, 19] cm

3 [3¼, 3¾, 3¾, 4, 4½]"
7.5 [8.5, 9.5, 9.5, 10, 11.5] cm

11 [12, 13¾, 15¼, 16¼, 17½]"
28 [30.5, 35, 38.5, 41.5, 44.5] cm

8 [8¼, 8½, 8¾, 9, 9¼]"
20.5 [21, 21.5, 22, 23, 23.5] cm

17"
43 cm

BODY, FRONTS
AND BACK

31½ [34¾, 38, 41¼, 44¼, 47½]"
80 [88, 96.5, 105, 112.5, 120.5] cm

SLEEVE

6½ [7, 7, 7¼, 7¾, 8]"
16.5 [18, 18, 18.5, 19.5, 20.5] cm

18"
45.5 cm

8¾ [8¾, 10, 11, 12, 13¼]"
22 [22, 25.5, 28, 30.5, 33.5] cm

Shape Neck

DEC ROW: (RS) Work to last 3 sts, ssp, p1—1 st dec'd.

NEXT ROW: Work even as est.

Rep the last 2 rows 7 (6, 5, 7, 6, 5) more times—14 (15, 17, 17, 18, 20) sts rem.

Cont to work even as est until armhole meas 7¾ (8, 8¼, 8½, 8¾, 9)" (19.5 [20.5, 21, 21.5, 22, 23] cm) from divide, ending with a RS row.

Shape Shoulder

Cont working as est, while shaping shoulder with short rows as foll:

SHORT ROW 1: (WS) Work to last 8 (9, 11, 12, 14, 16) sts, w&t (see Techniques).

SHORT ROW 2: (RS) Work to end.

SHORT ROW 3: Work to end of row, working wrap together with the st it wraps.

Sl all sts onto st holder or waste yarn. Break yarn and set aside.

Back

Return 57 (61, 67, 71, 75, 81) held back sts to larger cir and join yarn preparing to work a WS row.

Shape Armholes

(WS) Work 1 row.

DEC ROW: (RS) P1, p2tog, work to last 3 sts, ssp, p1—2 sts dec'd.

Rep the last 2 rows 2 (3, 4, 4, 5, 6) more times—51 (53, 57, 61, 63, 67) sts rem.

Work even until armholes measure 7¾ (8, 8¼, 8½, 8¾, 9)" (19.5 [20.5, 21, 21.5, 22, 23] cm) from divide, ending with a WS row.

Shape Shoulders

Cont working as est, while shaping shoulders with short rows as foll:

SHORT ROWS 1 AND 2: Work to last 8 (9, 11, 12, 14, 16) sts, w&t.

SHORT ROWS 3 AND 4: Work to end, working wrap together with the st it wraps.

Shape Neck

NEXT ROW: (RS) Work 14 (15, 17, 17, 18, 20) sts, BO 23 (23, 23, 27, 27, 27) sts for neck back, work across rem 14 (15, 17, 17, 18, 20) sts. Sl sts onto st holder or waste yarn. Break yarn leaving about 18" (45.5 cm) tail for three-needle BO.

Right Front

Return 29 (31, 34, 36, 38, 41) held right front sts to larger cir and join yarn preparing to work a WS row.

Shape Neck and Armhole

DEC ROW 1: (WS) Work to last 3 sts, k2tog, k1—28 (30, 33, 35, 37, 40) sts rem.

DEC ROW 2: (RS) P1, p2tog, work to last 3 sts, ssp, p1—2 sts dec'd.

NEXT ROW: Work even as est.

Rep the last 2 rows 2 (3, 4, 4, 5, 6) more times—22 (22, 23, 25, 25, 26) sts rem.

Shape Neck

DEC ROW: (RS) P1, p2tog, work to end—1 st dec'd.

NEXT ROW: Work even as est.

Rep the last 2 rows 7 (6, 5, 7, 6, 5) more times—14 (15, 17, 17, 18, 20) sts rem.

Cont to work even as est until armhole meas 7¾ (8, 8¼, 8½, 8¾, 9)" (19.5 [20.5, 21, 21.5, 22, 23] cm) from divide, ending with a WS row.

Shape Shoulder

Cont working as est, while shaping shoulder with short rows as foll:

SHORT ROW 1: (RS) Work to last 8 (9, 11, 12, 14, 16) sts, w&t (see Techniques).

SHORT ROW 2: (WS) Work to end.

SHORT ROW 3: Work to end of row, working wrap together with the st it wraps.

Sl sts onto st holder or waste yarn. Break yarn leaving about 18" (45.5 cm) tail for three-needle BO.

Shape Sleeve

INC RND: P1, M1P, work as est to end, M1P—2 sts inc'd.

Work 13 (11, 9, 7, 7, 7) rnds even as est.

Rep the last 14 (12, 10, 8, 8, 8) rnds 3 (5, 6, 7, 7, 7) more times—44 (48, 54, 60, 64, 68) sts.

Work even as est until sleeve meas 18" (45.5 cm) from beg, ending last rnd 3 (4, 4, 5, 6, 6) sts before m.

Shape Cap

BO the next 7 (9, 9, 11, 13, 13) sts—37 (39, 45, 49, 51, 55) sts rem.

Cont working back and forth in rows.

NEXT ROW: (WS) Work even as est.

DEC ROW: (RS) P1, p2tog, work as est to last 3 sts, ssp, p1—2 sts dec'd.

Rep the last 2 rows 2 (3, 4, 4, 5, 6) more times—31 (31, 35, 39, 39, 41) sts rem.

[Work 3 rows even, then rep dec row] 5 (5, 3, 2, 2, 1) times—21 (21, 29, 35, 35, 39) sts rem.

[Work 1 row even, then rep dec row] 3 (3, 5, 8, 8, 10) times—15 (15, 19, 19, 19, 19) sts rem.

DEC ROW: (WS) K1, ssk, work as est to last 3 sts, k2tog, k1—2 sts dec'd.

DEC ROW: (RS) P1, p2tog, work as est to last 3 sts, ssp, p1—2 sts dec'd.

Rep the last 2 rows 0 (0, 1, 1, 1, 1) more times, then work 1 more WS dec row—9 sts rem.

BO rem sts.

Finishing

Block pieces to measurements.

JOIN SHOULDERS: Return 14 (15, 17, 17, 18, 20) held sts from right front and right back onto larger dpn and with RS held together join sts using the three-needle BO (see Techniques). Rep for left shoulder.

With yarn threaded on a tapestry needle, sew sleeves into armholes.

Sleeve [make 2]

With smaller dpn, CO 36 (36, 40, 44, 48, 52) sts. Divide sts evenly over 3 or 4 dpn, pm for beg of rnd and join to work in the rnd, being careful not to twist sts.

Work k1, p1 rib until piece meas 3" (7.5 cm) from beg. Change to larger dpn.

EST PATT: Work 12 (12, 14, 16, 18, 20) sts in Rev St st, work 13 sts in Arts and Crafts Panel, work 11 (11, 13, 15, 17, 19) sts in Rev St st.

Cont working as est for 11 (11, 11, 5, 5, 5) more rnds.

NECKBAND: With smaller cir, and RS facing, beg at lower edge of right front, pick up and knit 68 sts to beg of neck shaping, 28 (30, 32, 34, 36, 38) sts evenly along right front neck to shoulder seam, pm, pick up and knit 23 (23, 23, 27, 27, 27) sts across back neck, pm, pick up and knit 28 (30, 32, 34, 36, 38) sts evenly along left front neck, then 68 sts to lower edge—215 (219, 223, 231, 235, 239) sts.

Shape Collar

Work in k1, p1 rib and shape using short rows as foll:

SHORT ROW 1: (WS) Work k1, p1 rib to second m, sl m, work 6 more sts in k1, p1 rib, w&t.

SHORT ROW 2: (RS) Work 35 (35, 35, 39, 39, 39) sts, w&t.

SHORT ROWS 3 AND 4: Work in k1, p1 rib to wrapped st, work the next st with the wrap, then work 3 (3, 3, 5, 5, 5) more sts, w&t.

SHORT ROWS 5 AND 6: Work in k1, p1 rib to wrapped st, work the next st with the wrap, then work 1 (3, 3, 3, 5, 5) sts w&t.

SHORT ROWS 7 AND 8: Work in k1, p1 rib to wrapped st, work the next st with the wrap, then work 1 (1, 3, 3, 3, 5) sts, w&t.

SHORT ROWS 9 AND 10: Work in k1, p1 rib to wrapped st, work the next st with the wrap, then work 1 st, w&t.

Rep the last 2 short rows 4 more times—71 (75, 79, 87, 91, 95) sts used for collar; 72 sts each side of wrapped sts.

NEXT ROW: (WS) Work k1, p1 rib to end.

Work 2 rows even in k1, p1 rib, ending with a WS row.

BUTTONHOLE ROW: (RS) [K1, p1] 2 times, ssk, [yo] twice, *[k1, p1] 7 times, ssk, [yo] twice; rep from * 3 more times, k1, [p1, k1] to end.

NEXT ROW: (WS) *Work in patt to double yo, purl into double yo dropping the extra wrap; rep from * 4 more times, work to end in patt.

Cont in patt for 2 more rows, ending with a WS row. BO all sts in patt.

Weave in loose ends. Sew buttons opposite buttonholes.

mucha CARDIGAN
Glenna Harris

Knit in pieces, seamed together, then topped with a short row collar, Glenna Harris's Art Nouveau-inspired kimono cardigan is an ode to one of the movement's shining lights, Alphonse Mucha. The back cabled panel conveys movement and fluidity, accompanied by a textured teardrop pattern reminiscent of the same organic shapes that grounded much of the movement. The combination of textural stitches, cables, and a draped style offers both contemporary versatility and classic comfort.

Finished measurements

About 41½ (47, 52, 58½)" (105.5 [119.5, 132, 148.5] cm) bust circumference.

Cardigan shown measures 41½" (105.5 cm) and is designed to be worn with 5–7" (12.5–18 cm) of positive ease.

Yarn

Worsted weight (#4 medium).

Shown here: Berroco Ultra Alpaca (50% super fine alpaca, 50% Peruvian wool; 215 yd [198 m]/100 g): #6253 dijon, 7 (8, 9, 10) skeins.

Needles

Lower Ribbing: Size U.S. 6 (4 mm): straight.

Body, Sleeves, and Collar: Size U.S. 7 (4.5 mm): straight.

Adjust needle sizes if necessary to obtain the correct gauge.

Notions

Markers (m); cable needle (cn); stitch holder or waste yarn; tapestry needle.

Gauge

17 sts and 27 rows = 4" (10 cm) in Seed Teardrop patt with larger needles.

29 sts between markers on back = 4¾" (12 cm) wide.

8 sts in Snake Cable charts = 1¼" (3.2 cm) wide.

Back

With smaller needle, CO 97 (109, 119, 133) sts.

EST RIBBING: (RS) P0 (2, 3, 2), [k2, p2] 9 (10, 11, 13) times, k4, [p2, k2] 2 times, p1, [k2, p2] 2 times, k4, [p2, k2] 9 (10, 11, 13) times, p0 (2, 3, 2).

NEXT ROW: (WS) K0 (2, 3, 2), [p2, k2] 9 (10, 11, 13) times, p4, [k2, p2] 2 times, k1, [p2, k2] 2 times, p4, [k2, p2] 9 (10, 11, 13) times, k0 (2, 3, 2).

Rep the last 2 rows 3 more times.

Change to larger needle.

EST PATT: (RS) K1 (edge st, keep in St st throughout), beg and end where indicated for right back, work 33 (39, 44, 51) sts in Seed Teardrop chart, pm, work 8 sts in Right Snake Cable chart, 13 sts in Large Cable chart, 8 sts in Left Snake Cable chart, pm, then beg and end where indicated for left back, work 33 (39, 44, 51) sts in Seed Teardrop chart, k1 (edge st, keep in St st throughout).

Cont as est until piece meas 17" (43 cm) from beg, ending with a WS row.

Shape Armholes

(RS) BO 3 (3, 4, 4) sts at beg of next 4 (4, 4, 6) rows—85 (97, 103, 109) sts rem.

Cont working even as est until armholes meas 8½ (9½, 10, 10½)" (21.5 [24, 25.5, 26.5] cm), ending with a WS row. BO all sts in patt.

Left Front

With smaller needle, CO 73 (79, 88, 95) sts.

EST RIB: (RS) P0 (2, 3, 2), [k2, p2] 9 (10, 11, 13) times, k4, [p2, k2] 8 (8, 9, 9) times, k1.

NEXT ROW: (WS) Sl 1 pwise wyf, [p2, k2] 8 (8, 9, 9) times, p4, [k2, p2] 9 (10, 11, 13) times, k0 (2, 3, 2).

Rep the last 2 rows 3 more times.

Change to larger needle.

EST PATT: (RS) K1 (edge st, keep in St st throughout), beg and end where indicated for left front, work 33 (39, 44, 51) sts in Seed Teardrop chart, pm, work 8 sts in Left Snake Cable chart, pm, [k2, p2] 7 (7, 8, 8) times, k3.

Cont working as est until piece meas 17" (43 cm) from beg, ending with a WS row.

(Note: Read the foll instructions carefully before cont; armhole and neck shaping beg at the same time.)

Shape Armhole

(RS) BO 3 (3, 4, 4) sts at beg of next 2 (2, 2, 3) RS rows; *at the same time,* on first RS row of armhole shaping, work neck shaping as foll:

Shape Neck

DEC ROW: (RS) Work as est to 3 sts before first m, k2tog, k1, sl m, work as est to end—1 st dec'd.

Work 1 row even as est.

Rep the last 2 rows 3 (5, 5, 5) more times—63 (67, 74, 77) sts rem.

[Rep dec row, then work 3 rows even] 4 (5, 5, 5) times—59 (62, 69, 72) sts rem.

Cont working even as est until armhole meas 8½ (9½, 10, 10½)" (21.5 [24, 25.5, 26.5] cm), ending with a RS row.

NEXT ROW: (WS) Work 31 (31, 35, 35) sts in rib as est, then place these sts onto a st holder or waste yarn for collar, BO rem 28 (31, 34, 37) sts in patt.

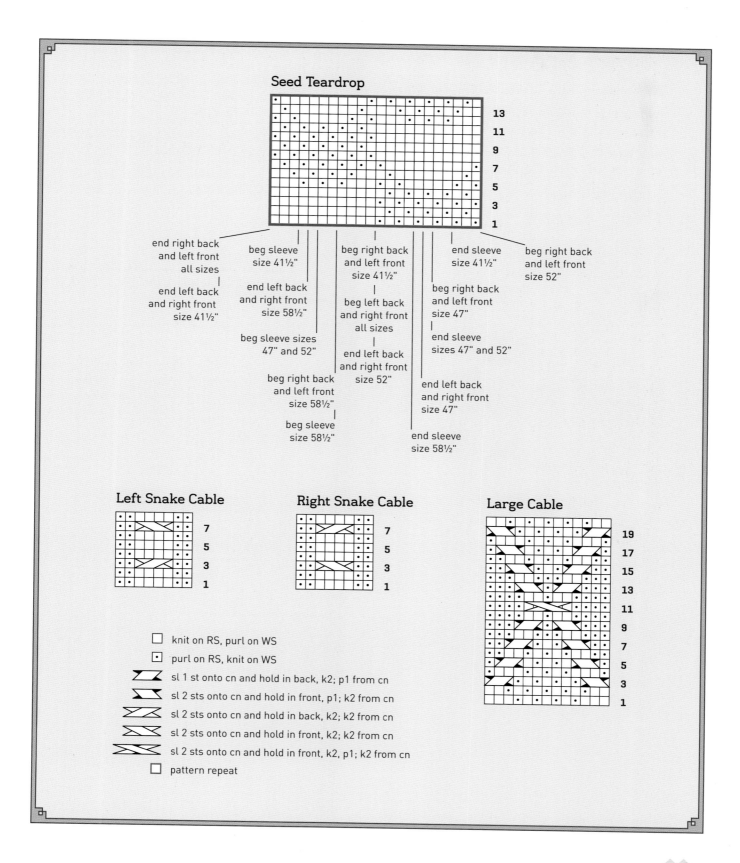

Seed Teardrop

13
11
9
7
5
3
1

end right back
and left front
all sizes

end left back
and right front
size 41½"

beg sleeve
size 41½"

end left back
and right front
size 58½"

beg sleeve sizes
47" and 52"

beg right back
and left front
size 58½"

beg sleeve
size 58½"

beg right back
and left front
size 41½"

beg left back
and right front
all sizes

end left back
and right front
size 52"

end sleeve
size 41½"

beg right back
and left front
size 47"

end sleeve
sizes 47" and 52"

end left back
and right front
size 47"

end sleeve
size 58½"

beg right back
and left front
size 52"

Left Snake Cable

7
5
3
1

Right Snake Cable

7
5
3
1

Large Cable

19
17
15
13
11
9
7
5
3
1

☐ knit on RS, purl on WS

⊡ purl on RS, knit on WS

sl 1 st onto cn and hold in back, k2; p1 from cn

sl 2 sts onto cn and hold in front, p1; k2 from cn

sl 2 sts onto cn and hold in back, k2; k2 from cn

sl 2 sts onto cn and hold in front, k2; k2 from cn

sl 2 sts onto cn and hold in front, k2, p1; k2 from cn

☐ pattern repeat

Right Front

With smaller needle, CO 73 (79, 88, 95) sts.

EST RIB: (RS) Sl 1 pwise wyb, [k2, p2] 8 (8, 9, 9) times, k4, [p2, k2] 9 (10, 11, 13) times, p0 (2, 3, 2).

NEXT ROW: (WS) K0 (2, 3, 2), [p2, k2] 9 (10, 11, 13) times, p4, [k2, p2] 8 (8, 9, 9) times, p1.

Rep the last 2 rows 3 more times.

Change to larger needle.

EST PATT: (RS) Sl 1 pwise wyb, [k2, p2] 7 (7, 8, 8) times, k2, pm, work 8 sts in Right Snake Cable chart, pm, beg and end where indicated for right front, work 33 (39, 44, 51) sts in Seed Teardrop chart, k1 (edge st, keep in St st throughout).

Cont working as est until piece meas 17" (43 cm) from beg, ending with a WS row.

*(**Note:** Read the foll instructions carefully before cont; armhole and neck shaping beg at the same time.)*

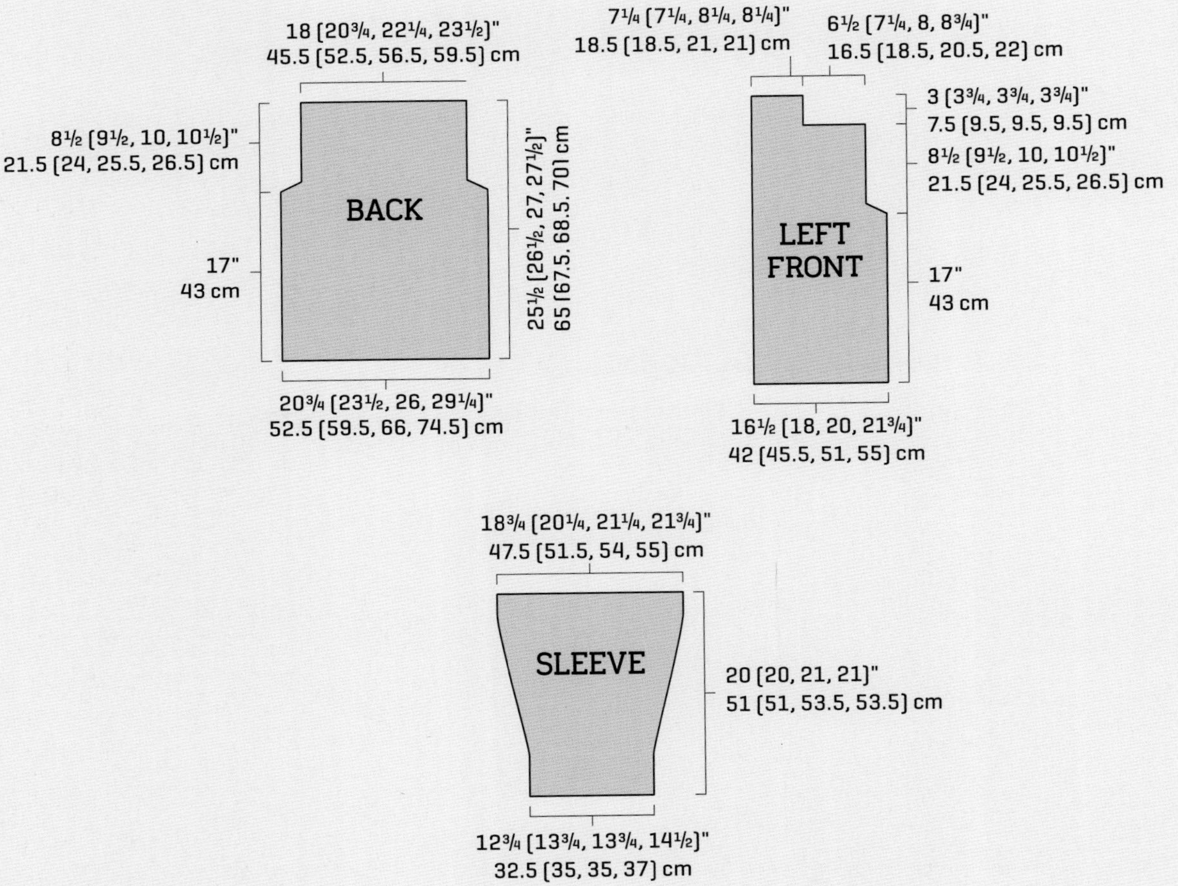

18 (20¾, 22¼, 23½)"
45.5 (52.5, 56.5, 59.5) cm
8½ (9½, 10, 10½)"
21.5 (24, 25.5, 26.5) cm
BACK
17"
43 cm
25½ (26½, 27, 27½)"
65 (67.5, 68.5, 70) cm
20¾ (23½, 26, 29¼)"
52.5 (59.5, 66, 74.5) cm
7¼ (7¼, 8¼, 8¼)"
18.5 (18.5, 21, 21) cm
6½ (7¼, 8, 8¾)"
16.5 (18.5, 20.5, 22) cm
3 (3¾, 3¾, 3¾)"
7.5 (9.5, 9.5, 9.5) cm
8½ (9½, 10, 10½)"
21.5 (24, 25.5, 26.5) cm
LEFT FRONT
17"
43 cm
16½ (18, 20, 21¾)"
42 (45.5, 51, 55) cm
18¾ (20¼, 21¼, 21¾)"
47.5 (51.5, 54, 55) cm
SLEEVE
20 (20, 21, 21)"
51 (51, 53.5, 53.5) cm
12¾ (13¾, 13¾, 14½)"
32.5 (35, 35, 37) cm

Shape Armhole

(WS) BO 3 (3, 4, 4) sts at beg of next 2 (2, 2, 3) WS rows; *at the same time*, on first RS row after beg of armhole shaping work neck shaping as foll:

Shape Neck

DEC ROW: (RS) Work as est to second m, sl m, k1, ssk (see Techniques), work as est to end—1 st dec'd.

Work 1 row even as est.

Rep the last 2 rows 3 (5, 5, 5) more times—63 (67, 74, 77) sts rem.

[Rep dec row, then work 3 rows even] 4 (5, 5, 5) times—59 (62, 69, 72) sts rem.

Cont working even as est until armhole meas 8½ (9½, 10, 10½)" (21.5 [24, 25.5, 26.5] cm), ending with a WS row.

NEXT ROW: (RS) Work 31 (31, 35, 35) sts in rib as est, then place these sts onto a st holder or waste yarn for collar, BO rem 28 (31, 34, 37) sts in patt.

Sleeve [make 2]

With smaller needle, CO 54 (58, 58, 62) sts.

EST RIB: (RS) K2, *p2, k2; rep from * to end.

NEXT ROW: (WS) P2, *k2, p2; rep from * to end.

Rep the last 2 rows 7 more times.

Change to larger needle.

EST PATT: (RS) K2 (edge sts, keep in St st throughout), beg and end where indicated for sleeve, work 50 (54, 54, 58) sts in Seed Teardrop chart, k2 (edge sts, keep in St st throughout).

Work even as est for 11 more rows, ending with a WS row.

Shape Sleeve

INC ROW: (RS) K2, M1 (see Techniques), work as est to last 2 sts, M1, k2—2 sts inc'd.

Work 5 rows even as est.

Rep the last 6 rows 3 (7, 13, 12) more times—62 (74, 86, 88) sts.

[Rep inc row, then work 7 rows even as est] 9 (6, 2, 2) times—80 (86, 90, 92) sts.

Cont working even as est until sleeve meas 20 (20, 21, 21)" (51 [51, 53.5, 53.5] cm) from beg, ending with a WS row. BO all sts in patt.

Finishing

Block pieces to measurements. Sew shoulder seams. Sew BO edge of sleeve along the straight edge of the armhole. Sew 1½ (1½, 2, 2¾)" (3.8 [3.8, 5, 7] cm) of the sleeve selvedge edges along the armhole BO sts. Sew sleeve and side seams.

Left Collar

Return 31 (31, 35, 35) held left front sts onto larger needle and join yarn preparing to work a RS row.

Shape Collar

Shape collar with short rows as foll, working wraps together with the st they wrap as you come to them:

ROW 1 AND ALL RS ROWS: Work as est to end.

ROW 2: (WS) Sl 1 pwise wyf, work 8 sts in rib as est, w&t (see Techniques).

ROW 4: Sl 1 pwise wyf, work 12 sts in rib as est, w&t.

ROW 6: Sl 1 pwise wyf, work 16 sts in rib as est, w&t.

ROW 8: Sl 1 pwise wyf, work 20 sts in rib as est, w&t.

ROW 10: Sl 1 pwise wyf, work 16 sts in rib as est, w&t.

ROW 12: Sl 1 pwise wyf, work 12 sts in rib as est, w&t.

ROW 14: Sl 1 pwise wyf, work 8 sts in rib as est, w&t.

Cont working even as est until collar meas 3 (3¾, 3¾, 3¾)" (7.5 [9.5, 9.5, 9.5] cm) from shoulder seam, or until it reaches the center of the back neck. Place sts onto st holder or waste yarn, cut yarn and set aside.

Right Collar

Return 31 (31, 35, 35) held right front sts onto larger needle and join yarn preparing to work a WS row.

Shape Collar

Shape collar with short rows as foll, working wraps together with the st they wrap as you come to them:

ROW 1 AND ALL WS ROWS: Work as est to end.

ROW 2: (RS) Sl 1 pwise wyb, work 8 sts in rib as est, w&t.

ROW 4: Sl 1 pwise wyb, work 12 sts in rib as est, w&t.

ROW 6: Sl 1 pwise wyb, work 16 sts in rib as est, w&t.

ROW 8: Sl 1 pwise wyb, work 20 sts in rib as est, w&t.

ROW 10: Sl 1 pwise wyb, work 16 sts in rib as est, w&t.

ROW 12: Sl 1 pwise wyb, work 12 sts in rib as est, w&t.

ROW 14: Sl 1 pwise wyb, work 8 sts in rib as est, w&t.

Cont working even as est until collar meas 3 (3¾, 3¾, 3¾)" (7.5 [9.5, 9.5, 9.5] cm) from shoulder seam, or until it reaches the center of the back neck. Return held left collar sts onto empty needle so tip is pointing in the same direction as the right collar needle. Holding pieces with RS's together, join sts using the three-needle BO (see Techniques). Sew edge of collar along back neck. Weave in ends.

beaux arts CARDIGAN
Cecily Glowik MacDonald

Cecily Glowik MacDonald's button-front cardigan is a wardrobe staple. Worked in the round to the armhole shaping, it sports elegant lace panels that flank the opening, bordered by a tidy I-cord edging. Slight waist shaping, ornate paneling, a garter collar, and matching button tabs against a background of simple stockinette embrace the idea that order and elegant details make for perfect harmony. These details call forth the Beaux Arts movement's love of symmetry.

Finished measurements

About 32 (34¼, 37¼, 39½, 42¾, 44¾, 48, 50¼, 53¼)" (81.5 [87, 94.5, 100.5, 108.5, 113.5, 122, 127.5, 135] cm) bust circumference, buttoned with 2 (1½, 2, 1½, 2, 1½, 2, 1½, 2)" (5 [3.8, 5, 3.8, 5, 3.8, 5, 3.8, 5] cm) gap between fronts.

Cardigan shown measures 34¼" (87 cm) and is designed to be worn with positive ease.

Yarn

Aran weight (#4 medium).

Shown here: Quince & Co. Osprey (100% American wool; 170 yd [155 m]/100 g): split pea, 5 (5, 6, 6, 6, 7, 7, 7, 8) skeins.

Needles

Body: Size U.S. 10 (6 mm): 29" (73.5 cm) circular (cir).

Sleeves: Size U.S. 10 (6 mm): set of 4 or 5 double-pointed (dpn).

Button Tabs: Size U.S. 9 (5.5 mm): straight.

Adjust needle sizes if necessary to obtain the correct gauge.

Notions

Markers (m); large stitch holders or waste yarn; four ⅞" (2.2 cm) buttons; tapestry needle.

Gauge

15 sts and 21 rows = 4" (10 cm) in St st with larger needles.

15 sts = 3¼" (8.5 cm) in Lace Panel with larger needles.

Stitch Guide

I-Cord Edging
(panel of 3 sts)

ROW 1: (WS) Sl 1 st pwise wyf, k1, sl 1 pwise wyf.

ROW 2: (RS) K1, sl 1 pwise wyf, k1.

Rep Rows 1 and 2 for patt.

Lace Panel
(panel of 15 sts)

(also, see chart)

ROW 1: (RS) P2, k2, k2tog, [k1, yo] twice, k1, ssk, k2, p2.

ROW 2: K4, p7, p4.

ROW 3: P2, k1, k2tog, k1, yo, k3, yo, k1, ssk, k1, p2.

ROW 4: K3, p9, k3.

ROW 5: P2, k2tog, k1, yo, k5, yo, k1, ssk, p2.

ROW 6: Rep Row 2.

ROW 7: P2, k11, p2.

ROW 8: K5, p5, k5.

Rep Rows 1–8 for patt.

Body

With cir needle, CO 118 (128, 138, 148, 158, 168, 178, 188, 198) sts. Do not join; work back and forth in rows.

PM FOR LACE AND SIDES: (WS) Work 3 sts in I-cord edging (see Stitch Guide), pm for Lace Panel, k15, pm for Lace Panel, k11 (14, 16, 19, 21, 24, 26, 29, 31), pm for side, k60 (64, 70, 74, 80, 84, 90, 94, 100), pm for side, k11 (14, 16, 19, 21, 24, 26, 29, 31), pm for Lace Panel, k15, pm for Lace Panel, work rem 3 sts in I-cord edging.

EST PATT: (RS) Work 3 sts in I-cord edging, sl m, work 15 sts in Lace Panel, sl m, work in Gtr st to next Lace Panel m, sl m, work 15 sts in Lace Panel, sl m, work 3 sts in I-cord edging.

Work as est for 5 more rows, ending with a WS row.

EST ST ST: (RS) Work 18 sts as est, sl m, work in St st to next Lace Panel m, sl m, work to end as est.

Cont to work even as est until piece meas 2¾" (7 cm) from beg, ending with a WS row.

Shape Waist

DEC ROW: (RS) *Work as est to 3 sts before side m, ssk, k1, sl m, k1, k2tog; rep from * once more, work to end as est—4 sts dec'd.

Work 9 rows even as est.

Rep the last 10 rows 2 more times—106 (116, 126, 136, 146, 156, 166, 176, 186) sts rem.

INC ROW: (RS) *Work to 2 sts before side m, RLI (see Techniques), k2, sl m, k1, RLI; rep from * once more, work to end as est—4 sts inc'd.

Work 9 rows even as est.

Rep the last 10 rows once more, then work Inc Row again—118 (128, 138, 148, 158, 168, 178, 188, 198) sts.

Work even as est until piece meas 15½ (15, 14¾, 14½, 14½, 14¼, 14, 13¾, 13½)" (39.5 [38, 37.5, 37, 37, 36, 35.5, 35, 34.5] cm) from beg, ending with a WS row.

DIVIDE FOR BACK AND FRONTS: (RS) *Work as est to 3 (3, 3, 4, 4, 4, 4, 5, 5) sts before side m, BO next 6 (6, 6, 8, 8, 8, 8, 10, 10) sts removing m; rep from * once more, work to end as est—26 (29, 31, 33, 35, 38, 40, 42, 44) sts rem each front, 54 (58, 64, 66, 72, 76, 82,

84, 90) sts rem for back. Place sts for right front and back onto st holders or waste yarn. Cont working back and forth in rows on left front sts only as foll:

Left Front
Shape Armhole

NEXT ROW: (WS) Work even as est.

DEC ROW: (RS) K1, ssk, work to end as est—1 st dec'd.

Rep the last 2 rows 4 (4, 4, 5, 6, 6, 7, 8, 9) more times—21 (24, 26, 27, 28, 31, 32, 33, 34) sts rem.

Cont working even as est until armhole meas 5 (5½, 5¾, 6, 6, 6¼, 6½, 6¾, 7)" (12.5 [14, 14.5, 15, 15, 16, 16.5, 17, 18] cm) from divide, ending with a RS row.

Shape Neck

NEXT ROW: (WS) Work 3 sts for I-cord edging and place those 3 sts onto a st holder or waste yarn, BO next 11 (12, 12, 12, 12, 13, 13, 13, 13) sts, p2 (1, 1, 1, 1, 0, 0, 0, 0), k2, work in St st to end—7 (9, 11, 12, 13, 15, 16, 17, 18) sts rem.

NEXT ROW: (RS) Work in St st to Lace Panel m, sl m, p2, k2 (1, 1, 1, 1, 0, 0, 0, 0) to end.

Cont working even as est until armhole meas 7½ (8, 8¼, 8½, 8½, 8¾, 9, 9¼, 9½)" (19 [20.5, 21, 21.5, 21.5, 22, 23, 23.5, 24] cm) from divide, ending with a WS row.

Shape Shoulder

ROW 1: (RS) BO 3 (4, 5, 6, 6, 7, 8, 8, 9) sts, work to end—4 (5, 6, 6, 7, 8, 9, 9) sts rem.

ROW 2: Work even as est.

ROW 3: BO rem 4 (5, 6, 6, 7, 8, 8, 9, 9) sts.

Back

Return 54 (58, 64, 66, 72, 76, 82, 84, 90) held back sts to cir needle and join yarn preparing to work a WS row.

Shape Armholes

NEXT ROW: (WS) Work even as est.

DEC ROW: (RS) K1, ssk, work to last 3 sts, k2tog, k1—2 sts dec'd.

Rep the last 2 rows 4 (4, 4, 5, 6, 6, 7, 8, 9) more times—44 (48, 54, 54, 58, 62, 66, 66, 70) sts rem.

Cont working even in St st until armhole meas 7½ (8, 8¼, 8½, 8½, 8¾, 9, 9¼, 9½)" (19 [20.5, 21, 21.5, 21.5, 22, 23, 23.5, 24] cm) from divide, ending with a WS row.

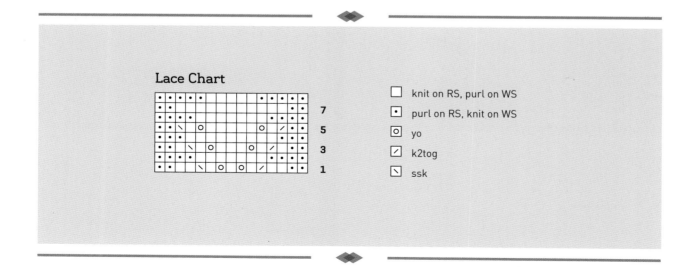

Lace Chart

	knit on RS, purl on WS
•	purl on RS, knit on WS
O	yo
⁄	k2tog
\	ssk

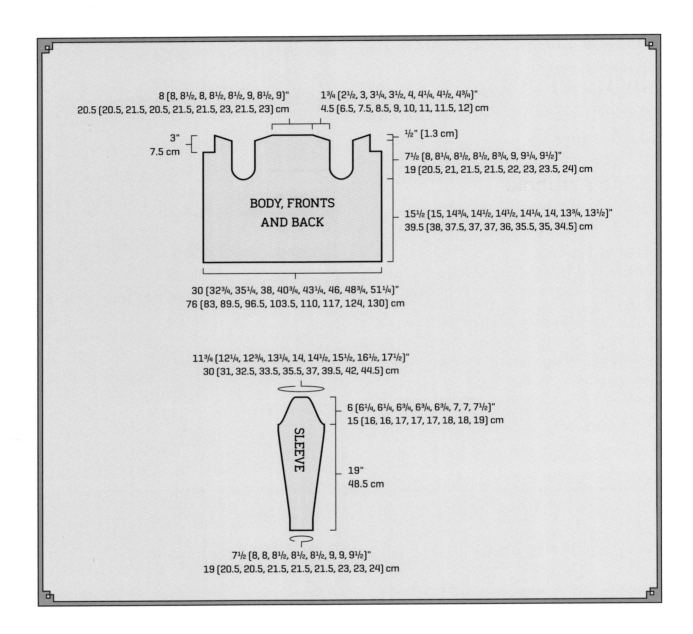

8 [8, 8½, 8, 8½, 8½, 9, 8½, 9]"
20.5 [20.5, 21.5, 20.5, 21.5, 21.5, 23, 21.5, 23] cm

1¾ [2½, 3, 3¼, 3½, 4, 4¼, 4½, 4¾]"
4.5 [6.5, 7.5, 8.5, 9, 10, 11, 11.5, 12] cm

3"
7.5 cm

½" [1.3 cm]

7½ [8, 8¼, 8½, 8½, 8¾, 9, 9¼, 9½]"
19 [20.5, 21, 21.5, 21.5, 22, 23, 23.5, 24] cm

BODY, FRONTS
AND BACK

15½ [15, 14¾, 14½, 14½, 14¼, 14, 13¾, 13½]"
39.5 [38, 37.5, 37, 37, 36, 35.5, 35, 34.5] cm

30 [32¾, 35¼, 38, 40¾, 43¼, 46, 48¾, 51¼]"
76 [83, 89.5, 96.5, 103.5, 110, 117, 124, 130] cm

11¾ [12¼, 12¾, 13¼, 14, 14½, 15½, 16½, 17½]"
30 [31, 32.5, 33.5, 35.5, 37, 39.5, 42, 44.5] cm

6 [6¼, 6¼, 6¾, 6¾, 6¾, 7, 7, 7½]"
15 [16, 16, 17, 17, 17, 18, 18, 19] cm

SLEEVE

19"
48.5 cm

7½ [8, 8, 8½, 8½, 8½, 9, 9, 9½]"
19 [20.5, 20.5, 21.5, 21.5, 21.5, 23, 23, 24] cm

Shape Shoulders

BO 3 (4, 5, 6, 6, 7, 8, 8, 9) sts at beg of next 2 rows, then BO 4 (5, 6, 6, 7, 8, 8, 9, 9) sts at the beg of the foll 2 rows—30 (30, 32, 30, 32, 32, 34, 32, 34) sts rem. BO rem sts.

Right Front

Return 26 (29, 31, 33, 35, 38, 40, 42, 44) held right front sts to cir needle and join yarn preparing to work a WS row.

Shape Armhole

NEXT ROW: (WS) Work even as est.

DEC ROW: (RS) Work as est to last 3 sts, k2tog, k1—1 st dec'd.

Rep the last 2 rows 4 (4, 4, 5, 6, 6, 7, 8, 9) more times—21 (24, 26, 27, 28, 31, 32, 33, 34) sts rem.

Cont working even until armhole meas 5 (5½, 5¾, 6, 6, 6¼, 6½, 6¾, 7)" (12.5 [14, 14.5, 15, 15, 16, 16.5, 17, 18] cm) from divide, ending with a WS row.

Shape Neck

NEXT ROW: (RS) Work 3 sts for I-cord edging and place those 3 sts onto a st holder or waste yarn, BO next 11 (12, 12, 12, 12, 13, 13, 13, 13) sts, k2 (1, 1, 1, 1, 0, 0, 0, 0), p2, work in St st to end—7 (9, 11, 12, 13, 15, 16, 17, 18) sts rem.

NEXT ROW: (WS) Work in St st to Lace Panel m, sl m, k2, p2 (1, 1, 1, 1, 0, 0, 0, 0) to end.

Cont working even as est until armhole meas 7½ (8, 8¼, 8½, 8½, 8¾, 9, 9¼, 9½)" (19 [20.5, 21, 21.5, 21.5, 22, 23, 23.5, 24] cm) from divide, ending with a RS row.

Shape Shoulder

ROW 1: (WS) BO 3 (4, 5, 6, 6, 7, 8, 8, 9) sts, work to end—4 (5, 6, 6, 7, 8, 8, 9, 9) sts rem.

ROW 2: Work even as est.

ROW 3: BO rem 4 (5, 6, 6, 7, 8, 8, 9, 9) sts.

Sleeve [make 2]

CO 28 (30, 30, 32, 32, 32, 34, 34, 36) sts. Divide sts evenly over 3 or 4 dpn. Pm for beg of rnd and join to work in the rnd, being careful not to twist sts.

[Purl 1 rnd, knit 1 rnd] 2 times. Purl 1 rnd.

Work even in St st until piece meas 1¼" (3.2 cm) from beg.

Shape Sleeve

INC RND: K1, RLI , knit to last 2 sts, RLI, k2—2 sts inc'd.

[Work 11 (11, 9, 9, 7, 7, 5, 5, 5) rnds even, then rep Inc Rnd] 7 (7, 6, 6, 3, 8, 2, 10, 12) times—44 (46, 44, 46, 40, 50, 40, 56, 62) sts.

Sizes 37¼ (39½, 42¾, 44¾, 48, 50¼, 53¼)" only:

[Work 11 (11, 9, 9, 7, 7, 7) rnds even, then rep Inc Rnd] 2 (2, 6, 2, 9, 3, 2) times—48 (50, 52, 54, 58, 62, 66) sts.

All sizes:

Cont working even until piece meas 19" (48.5 cm) from beg, ending last rnd 3 (3, 3, 4, 4, 4, 4, 5, 5) sts before m.

Shape Cap

NEXT RND: BO 6 (6, 6, 8, 8, 8, 8, 10, 10) sts, k1, ssk, knit to last 3 sts, k2tog, k1—36 (38, 40, 40, 42, 44, 48, 50, 54) sts rem. Cont working back and forth in rows as foll:

NEXT ROW: Purl.

DEC ROW: (RS) K1, ssk, knit to last 3 sts, k2tog, k1—2 sts dec'd.

Rep the last 2 rows 6 (7, 9, 8, 8, 7, 10, 12, 15) more times—22 (22, 20, 22, 24, 28, 26, 24, 22) sts rem.

[Work 3 rows even, then rep Dec Row] 3 (3, 2, 3, 3, 3, 2, 1, 0) times—16 (16, 16, 16, 18, 22, 22, 22, 22) sts rem.

DEC ROW: (WS) P1, p2tog, purl to last 3 sts, ssp (see Techniques), p1—2 sts dec'd.

DEC ROW: (RS) K1, ssk, knit to last 3 sts, k2tog, k1—2 sts dec'd.

Rep the last 2 rows 1 (1, 1, 1, 2, 2, 2, 2) more times—8 (8, 8, 8, 10, 10, 10, 10, 10) sts rem.

Finishing

Block pieces to measurements. Set in sleeves.

COLLAR: With RS facing, return 3 held right front I-cord edging sts to cir needle, pick up and knit 11 (12, 12, 12, 12, 13, 13, 13, 13) sts along BO sts, 11 sts evenly along right front neck edge, 30 (30, 32, 30, 32, 32, 34, 32, 34) sts along back neck, 11 sts evenly along left front neck edge, then 11 (12, 12, 12, 12, 13, 13, 13, 13) sts along BO sts, place 3 held left front I-cord edging sts onto empty end of needle and work in I-cord edging—80 (82, 84, 82, 84, 86, 88, 86, 88) sts.

EST PATT: (WS) Work 3 sts in I-cord edging as est, work to last 3 sts in Gtr st, work last 3 sts in I-cord edging as est.

Cont working as est for 2" (5 cm), ending with a RS row. BO all sts in patt.

Button Tabs (make 2)

With smaller needles, CO 5 sts.

Knit 2 rows.

BUTTONHOLE ROW: (RS) K2, yo, k2tog, k1.

Knit 13 (11, 13, 11, 13, 11, 13, 11, 13) rows, ending with a WS row.

Rep Buttonhole Row.

Knit 2 rows.

BO all sts kwise.

Sew 2 buttons onto each front 1" (2.5 cm) from the edge, the first in the center of the collar, and the second 3" (7.5 cm) below the first.

Get Inspired

A style taught at the famous École des Beaux-Arts in Paris, the Beaux Arts movement was prevalent from 1885 to 1920. Featuring bold lines, symmetry, oversized ornate details, and bas-relief panels, this style was usually confined to large buildings such as train stations, courthouses, opera houses, and museums. Its combination of Greek and Roman ideals with Italian Renaissance forms is often referred to as "American Renaissance," recalling a time when the United States looked to Europe for trends.

persian SHAWL
Kirsten Kapur

This oversized, horizontal-knit shawl by Kirsten Kapur embodies what Persian architecture has in abundance—high arches, columns, and recesses reflected in the lace pattern. The blue is referred to as "Persian blue," a color that is found in Persian pottery, mosques, and tiles.

Finished measurements
About 22¼" (56.5 cm) tall × 90" (228.5 cm) long.

Yarn
DK weight (#3 light).

Shown here: Hazel Knits DK Lively (90% superwash merino, 10% nylon; 275 yd [251 m]/140 g): #232 wheatberry (MC), 3 skeins; #222 jay blue (CC), 1 skein.

Needles
Size U.S. 10 (6 mm): 40" (100 cm) circular (cir).

Adjust needle size if necessary to obtain the correct gauge.

Notions
Markers (m); tapestry needle.

Gauge
12½ sts and 23 rows = 4" (10 cm) in Shawl Charts A–D.

Notes: Circular needle is used to accommodate large number of sts. Do not join; work back and forth in rows.

Border

With MC, CO 281 sts.

Knit 1 WS row.

Est Mosaic Patt

ROW 1: (RS) With CC, k1, *sl 1 pwise wyb, k1; rep from * to end.

ROW 2: (WS) With CC, k1, *sl 1 pwise wyf, k1; rep from * to end.

ROWS 3 AND 4: With MC, knit.

ROWS 5 AND 6: With CC, knit.

ROWS 7 AND 8: With MC, knit.

Rep the last 8 rows 3 more times.

Cut CC leaving an 8" (20.5 cm) tail.

Body

Cont working with MC only.

ROW 1: (RS) Knit.

ROW 2: K56, pm, k169, pm, k56.

ROW 3: Knit to first m, sl m, k1, *yo, k2tog, yo, k3, s2kp (see Techniques), k3, yo, ssk (see Techniques), yo, k1; rep from * to next m, remove m, w&t (see Techniques).

ROW 4: Purl to m, remove m, w&t.

Cont working from the charts as foll:

Work Rows 3–16 of Shawl Chart A, Rows 1–16 of Shawl Charts B and C, Rows 1–8 of Shawl Chart D, then Rows 1–16 of Shawl Charts A, B, and C.

Shawl Chart A

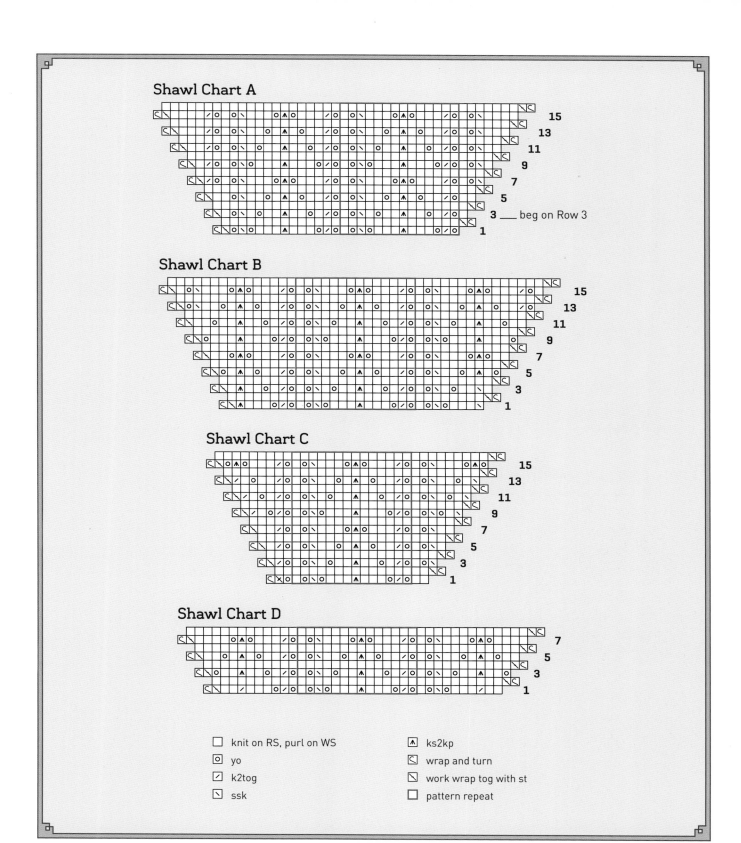

Shawl Chart B

Shawl Chart C

Shawl Chart D

	knit on RS, purl on WS		ks2kp
	yo		wrap and turn
	k2tog		work wrap tog with st
	ssk		pattern repeat

Get Inspired

In an area of the world that has had much conflict, Persian or Iranian architecture has remained virtually unchanged since around 5000 B.C. Made from materials straight from the earth such as clay and brick, and featuring heavy religious symbolism through simple shapes such as circles and squares, structures in this style are often massive in size with an ornate interior.

Top Edge

ROWS 1 AND 2: With CC, knit to the last wrapped st, knit the st together with the wrap, w&t.

ROWS 3 AND 4: With MC, knit to the last wrapped st, knit the st together with the wrap, w&t.

ROWS 5–9: With CC, knit to the last wrapped st, knit the st together with the wrap, w&t.

With CC, BO all sts loosely.

Finishing

Weave in ends. Block by soaking in cool water, wrap in towel to gently wring out excess water. Pin to measurements.

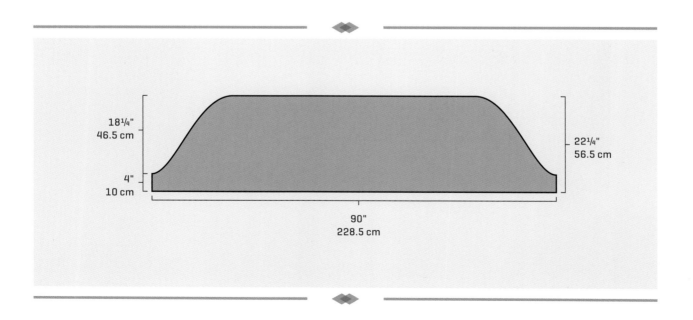

18¼"
46.5 cm

4"
10 cm

22¼"
56.5 cm

90"
228.5 cm

byzantine PULLOVER
Tanis Lavallée

Knit in the round from the top down, Tanis Lavallée's Fair Isle yoke pullover is a work of art not unlike the Byzantine mosaics that inspired it. Knit in a traditional stranded technique with five colors, the Fair Isle pattern is based on mosaics that often depicted a religious or political scene or a complex geometric design. These mosaics achieved a glowing effect due to their construction from bits of glass, stone, marble, or gold leaf sandwiched between glass.

Finished measurements
About 28¾ (32¾, 36½, 40¼, 44¼, 48)" (73 [83, 92.5, 102, 112.5, 122] cm) bust circumference.

Pullover shown measures 36½" (92.5 cm) and is designed to fit with little or no ease.

Yarn
Sock weight (#2 super fine).

Shown here: Tanis Fiber Arts Purple Label Cashmere Sock (70% merino, 20% cashmere, 10% nylon; 400 yd [365 m]/115 g): sand (A), 3 (3, 4, 4, 5, 5) skeins; peacock (B), deep sea (C), garnet (D), and gold (E), 1 skein each.

Needles
Size U.S. 4 (3.5 mm): 16" and 32" (40 and 80 cm) circular (cir) and set of 4 or 5 double-pointed (dpn).

Adjust needle size if necessary to obtain the correct gauge.

Notions
Markers (m); stitch holders or waste yarn; tapestry needle.

Gauge
25 sts and 36 rnds = 4" (10 cm) in St st, worked in rnds.

Yoke

With 16" cir or dpn and A, loosely CO 104 (114, 114, 129, 143, 158) sts. Pm and join for working in the rnd, being careful not to twist sts.

Work in twisted rib (see Stitch Guide) until piece meas 1" (2.5 cm) from beg.

Knit 1 rnd.

INC RND 1: *K4 (3, 2, 2, 2, 2), M1 (see Techniques); rep from * to last 4 (6, 0, 1, 1, 2) sts, knit to end—129 (150, 171, 193, 214, 236) sts.

Work even in St st until piece meas 2¼ (2½, 3, 3¼, 3½, 3¾)" (5.5 [6.5, 7.5, 8.5, 9, 9.5] cm) from beg.

INC RND 2: *K3, M1; rep from * to last 3 (0, 0, 1, 1, 2) sts, knit to end—171 (200, 228, 257, 285, 314) sts.

Work even in St st until piece meas 3¼ (4, 5, 5¼, 6, 6¾)" (8.5 [10, 12.5, 13.5, 15, 17] cm) from beg.

INC RND 3: *K3, M1; rep from * to last 0 (2, 0, 2, 0, 2) sts, knit to end—228 (266, 304, 342, 380, 418) sts.

Knit 1 rnd.

Work Rnds 1–41 of Yoke chart.

With A only, knit 1 rnd even.

DIVIDE FOR SLEEVES: Remove beg of rnd m, *k70 (80, 92, 102, 114, 126) sts for back, sl next 44 (53, 60, 69, 76, 83) sts onto st holder or waste yarn for sleeve, use the backward loop method to CO 10 (11, 11, 12, 12, 12) sts, pm for side, CO another 10 (11, 11, 12, 12, 12) sts; rep from * once more for front—180 (204, 228, 252, 276, 300) sts rem. The second marker placed is the new beg of rnd m.

Body

Work even in St st until piece meas 2" (5 cm) from divide.

Shape Waist

DEC RND: *K2, k2tog, knit to 4 sts before m, ssk, k2, sl m; rep from * once more—4 sts dec'd.

Knit 9 rnds.

Rep the last 10 rnds 2 more times—168 (192, 216, 240, 264, 288) sts rem.

Knit 1 rnd.

INC RND: *K2, M1, knit to 2 sts before m, M1, k2, sl m; rep from * once more—4 sts inc'd.

Knit 9 rnds.

Rep the last 10 rnds 2 more times—180 (204, 228, 252, 276, 300) sts.

Work even in St st until piece meas 13 (14, 14, 15, 15, 16). (33 [35.5, 35.5, 38, 38, 40.5] cm) from divide.

TURNING RND: Purl.

Change to E and work in St st for 1¼" (3.2 cm). BO all sts loosely.

Yoke Chart

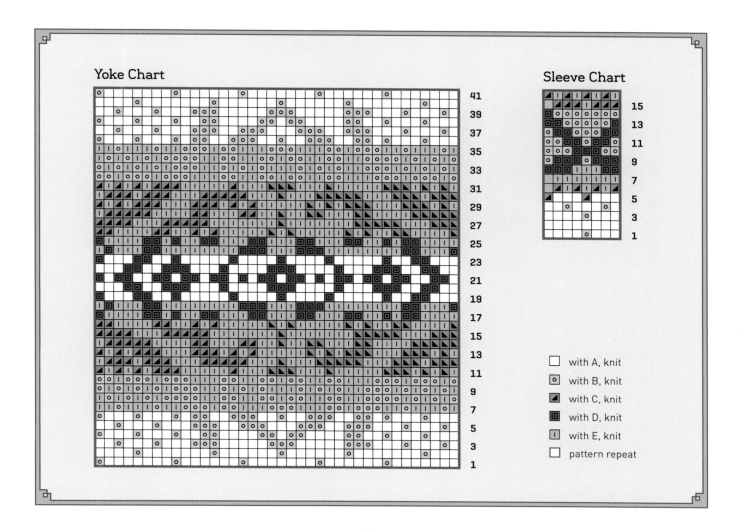

41
39
37
35
33
31
29
27
25
23
21
19
17
15
13
11
9
7
5
3
1

Sleeve Chart

15
13
11
9
7
5
3
1

	with A, knit
	with B, knit
	with C, knit
	with D, knit
	with E, knit
	pattern repeat

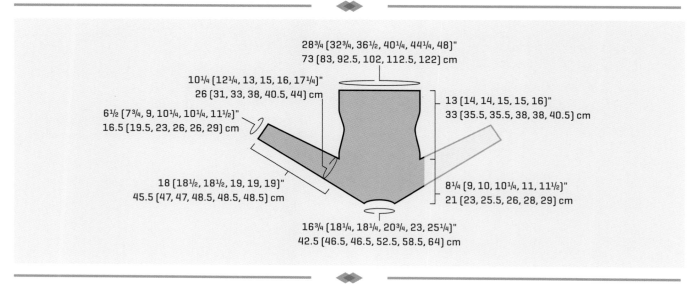

28³⁄₄ [32³⁄₄, 36¹⁄₂, 40¹⁄₄, 44¹⁄₄, 48]"
73 [83, 92.5, 102, 112.5, 122] cm

10¹⁄₄ [12¹⁄₄, 13, 15, 16, 17¹⁄₄]"
26 [31, 33, 38, 40.5, 44] cm

6¹⁄₂ [7³⁄₄, 9, 10¹⁄₄, 10¹⁄₄, 11¹⁄₂]"
16.5 [19.5, 23, 26, 26, 29] cm

13 [14, 14, 15, 15, 16]"
33 [35.5, 35.5, 38, 38, 40.5] cm

18 [18¹⁄₂, 18¹⁄₂, 19, 19, 19]"
45.5 [47, 47, 48.5, 48.5, 48.5] cm

8¹⁄₄ [9, 10, 10¹⁄₄, 11, 11¹⁄₂]"
21 [23, 25.5, 26, 28, 29] cm

16³⁄₄ [18¹⁄₄, 18¹⁄₄, 20³⁄₄, 23, 25¹⁄₄]"
42.5 [46.5, 46.5, 52.5, 58.5, 64] cm

Evolving from Roman architecture, the Byzantine style emerged from the new capital of Constantinople. Using materials such as stone, mosaic, and alabaster, and new ideas in building, such as domes, semidomes, and differently shaped floor plans, this era is an important stepping-stone to the Gothic style. The art inside Byzantine structures was something very new at the time. Letting go of literal artwork, this style introduced abstract images and combined politics and religion, two things that were rarely mixed at the time.

Sleeve

Return 44 (53, 60, 69, 76, 83) held sleeve sts evenly spaced onto dpns. Beg at center of underarm CO sts, with A pick up and knit 10 (11, 11, 12, 12, 12) sts from first half of CO sts, knit to end, pick up and knit 10 (11, 11, 12, 12, 12) sts from rem CO sts, pm for beg of rnd—64 (75, 82, 93, 100, 107) sts.

Sizes 32¾ (40¼, 48)" only:

INC RND: M1 , knit to end—76 (94, 108) sts rem.

All sizes:

Work in St st until piece meas 4" (10 cm) from underarm.

Shape Sleeve

DEC RND: K2, k2tog, knit to 4 sts before marker, ssk, k2—2 sts dec'd.

Knit 6 (5, 6, 5, 4, 4) rnds.

Rep the last 7 (6, 7, 6, 5, 5) rnds 11 (13, 12, 14, 17, 17) more times—40 (48, 56, 64, 64, 72) sts rem.

Cont working even in St st until piece meas 14½ (15, 15, 15½, 15½, 15½)" (37 [38, 38, 39.5, 39.5, 39.5] cm) from underarm, or 3½" (9 cm) shorter than desired sleeve length.

Work Rnds 1–16 of Sleeve chart.

Knit 2 rnds.

Work in twisted rib for 1½" (3.8 cm). BO all sts loosely in patt.

Finishing

Turn body hem to WS at turning rnd and sew in place. Weave in ends and block to measurements.

fisher building MITTENS

Jane Dupuis

Jane Dupuis's Fisher Building mittens are worked in a traditional stranded Fair Isle technique. They are knit from the bottom up in the round, with an afterthought thumb and symmetrical decreasing at the top. With different motifs on the outside and inside of the mitt, this gorgeous pair evokes the geometric designs seen often in the Art Deco period.

Finished measurements

About 8¾" (22 cm) hand circumference × 9¾" (25 cm) long.

Yarn

Sock weight (#1 super fine).

Shown here: Lorna's Laces Shepherd Sock (80% superwash merino wool, 20% nylon; 430 yd [393 m]/100 g): aqua (A), patina (B), 1 skein each.

Needles

Size U.S. 1 (2.25 mm): set of 5 double-pointed (dpn).

Adjust needle size if necessary to obtain the correct gauge.

Notions

Marker (m); waste yarn; tapestry needle.

Gauge

33 sts and 35 rnds = 4" (10 cm) in Mitten chart, worked in rnds.

Left Mitten Cuff

With B, use the long-tail method (see Techniques) or any stretchy method to CO 72. Distribute sts evenly over 4 dpn (18 sts on each). The needles will now be known as Needles 1, 2, 3, and 4, respectively. Pm for beg of rnd and join to work in the rnd, being careful not to twist sts.

EST RIBBING: *K2tbl, p2; rep from *.

Cont working as est for 9 more rnds.

Left Mitten Body

Change to A and knit 2 rnds.

Work Rnds 1–29 of Mitten chart.

Piece should meas about 4½" (11.5 cm) to here.

Left Thumb Placement

Work Rnd 30 of Mitten chart across all sts on Needles 1, 2, and 3 (54 sts); on Needle 4: k3, using a 10" (25.5 cm) piece of waste yarn k12, sl these 12 sts back onto the left needle and knit to end in patt.

Work Rnds 31–62 of Mitten chart.

Piece should meas about 8¼" (21 cm) to here.

Shape Fingers

Cont to work Rnds 63–76 of Mitten chart—16 sts rem (4 sts on each needle).

Sl 4 sts from Needle 2 onto Needle 1, and 4 sts from Needle 4 onto Needle 3 (8 sts on 2 needles). Break yarn A, leaving about 12" (30.5 cm) tail. With tail threaded on tapestry needle and holding needles with WS's together, join sts using the Kitchener st (see Techniques).

Thumb

Carefully remove waste yarn from the thumb placement section and place 12 sts from above and below each onto a dpn—24 sts. Divide sts evenly over 4 dpn (6 sts on each). Pm for beg of rnd.

Mitten Chart

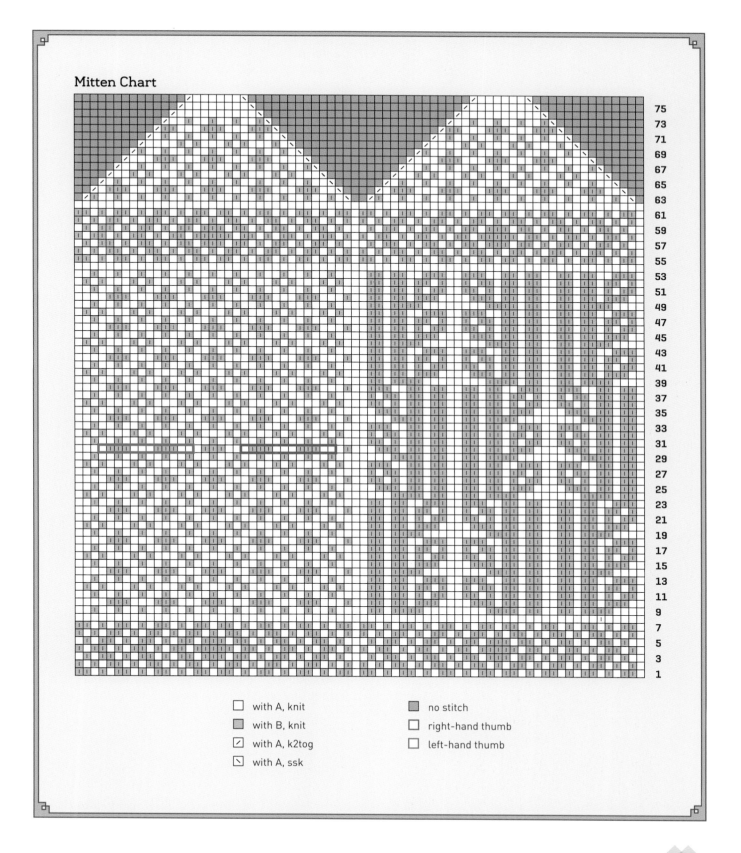

75
73
71
69
67
65
63
61
59
57
55
53
51
49
47
45
43
41
39
37
35
33
31
29
27
25
23
21
19
17
15
13
11
9
7
5
3
1

☐ with A, knit
▨ with B, knit
☑ with A, k2tog
☒ with A, ssk

▨ no stitch
☐ right-hand thumb
☐ left-hand thumb

Get Inspired

Completed in 1928 in Detroit, the thirty-story-high Fisher Building is a classic example of Art Deco architecture, with a stair-stepped exterior and ornate detailing. Housing a large barrel-vaulted lobby, opera house, and twenty-one elevators, and originally covered in golden tiles (later painted green during WWII to detract attention from bombers), the building was originally home to Fisher Body Company, a car body business acquired by General Motors.

INC RND: With A and RS facing, beg at one end of thumb, *with Needle 1: pick up and knit 1 st, k6; with Needle 2: k6, pick up and knit 1 st; rep from * for Needles 3 and 4—28 sts (7 sts on each needle).

Cont working in St st until thumb meas 2" (5 cm) from pick-up rnd or ½" (1.3 cm) less than desired total length.

Shape Thumb

DEC RND: *On Needle 1: ssk, knit to end of needle; on Needle 2: knit to last 2 sts, k2tog; rep from * for Needles 3 and 4—4 sts dec'd.

Rep the last rnd 4 more times—8 sts rem (2 sts on each needle).

Break yarn leaving a tail about 4" (10 cm) long. With tail threaded on tapestry needle, thread through all sts and pull tightly to close top of thumb.

Right Mitten

Work Cuff and Body same as for left mitten to the thumb placement.

Right Thumb Placement

Work Rnd 30 of Mitten chart across all sts on Needles 1 and 2 (36 sts); on Needle 3: k3, using a 10" (25.5 cm) piece of waste yarn k12, sl these 12 sts back onto the left needle and knit to end in patt; on Needle 4: work Rnd 30 across all 18 sts.

Cont working same as for left mitten.

Finishing

Weave in ends.

Place mittens beneath a damp tea towel and press with a hot iron to steam block.

rococo MITTENS
Jane Dupuis

Knit from the bottom up in the round, with an afterthought thumb and symmetrical decreasing at the top, Jane Dupuis's Rococo mittens are worked in a traditional stranded Fair Isle technique. When the wearer joins their hands together, a flourishing, ornate design runs across both mittens. This playfulness and clever design are hallmarks of this period.

Finished measurements

About 8" (20.5 cm) hand circumference × 10¼" (26 cm) long.

Yarn

Sock weight (#1 super fine).

Shown here: Lorna's Laces Shepherd Sock (80% superwash merino wool, 20% nylon; 430 yd [393 m]/100 g): pond blue (A), natural (B), 1 skein each.

Needles

Size U.S. 2 (2.75 mm): set of 5 double-pointed (dpn).

Adjust needle size if necessary to obtain the correct gauge.

Notions

Marker (m); waste yarn; tapestry needle.

Gauge

32 sts and 32 rnds = 4" (10 cm) in Left and Right Mitten charts, worked in rnds.

Left Mitten Cuff

With B, use the long-tail method (see Techniques) or any stretchy method to CO 64 sts. Distribute sts evenly over 4 dpn (16 sts on each). The needles will now be known as Needles 1, 2, 3, and 4, respectively. Pm for beg of rnd and join to work in the rnd, being careful not to twist the sts.

EST RIBBING: *K2tbl, p2; rep from *.

Cont working as est for 9 more rnds.

Left Mitten Body

Work Rnds 1–29 of Left Mitten chart.

Piece should meas about 4¾" (12 cm) to here.

Left Thumb Placement

Work Rnd 30 across all sts on Needles 1, 2, and 3 (48 sts); on Needle 4: k3, using a 10" (25.5 cm) piece of waste yarn k10, sl these 10 sts back onto the left needle and knit to end in patt.

Work Rnds 31–60 of Left Mitten chart.

Piece should meas about 8½" (21.5 cm) to here.

Shape Fingers

Cont to work Rnds 61–74 of Left Mitten chart—8 sts rem (2 sts on each needle).

Break yarn A, leaving a tail about 4" (10 cm) long. With tail threaded on tapestry needle, thread through all sts and pull tightly to close top.

Thumb

Carefully remove waste yarn from the thumb placement section and place 10 sts from above and below each onto a dpn—20 sts. Divide sts evenly over 4 dpn (5 sts on each). Pm for beg of rnd.

INC RND: With A and RS facing, beg at one end of thumb, *with Needle 1 pick up and knit 1 st, k5; with Needle 2 k5, pick up and knit 1 st; rep from * for Needles 3 and 4—24 sts (6 sts on each needle).

Cont working in St st until thumb meas 2" (5 cm) from pick-up rnd or ½" (1.3 cm) less than desired total length.

Shape Thumb

DEC RND: *On Needle 1: ssk, knit to end of needle; on Needle 2: knit to last 2 sts, k2tog; rep from * for Needles 3 and 4—4 sts dec'd.

Rep the last rnd 3 more times—8 sts rem (2 sts on each needle).

Break yarn leaving a tail about 4" (10 cm) long. With tail threaded on tapestry needle, thread through all sts and pull tightly to close top of thumb.

Right Mitten

Work cuff and body same as for left mitten to thumb placement, working Right Mitten chart in place of Left Mitten chart.

Right Thumb Placement

Work Rnd 3 across the first 3 sts on Needle 1, using a 10" (25.5 cm) piece of waste yarn k10, sl these 10 sts back onto the left needle and knit to end in patt; on Needles 2, 3, and 4: work Rnd 30 to end.

Cont working same as for left mitten, working Right Mitten chart in place of Left Mitten chart.

Finishing

Weave in ends.

Place mittens beneath a damp tea towel and press with a hot iron to steam block.

Get Inspired

Its name derived from a French word combining "stone" and "shell," two motifs found often in the period, Rococo style flourished in Europe in the early eighteenth century. The trademarks of Rococo are soft colors, gold, ornate details, and asymmetry, and can be spied in paintings, sculptures, buildings, gardens, jewelry, and even clothing of the period. Buildings and rooms done in this time were often seen as one complete work of art, rather than individual items making up a space.

Left Mitten Chart

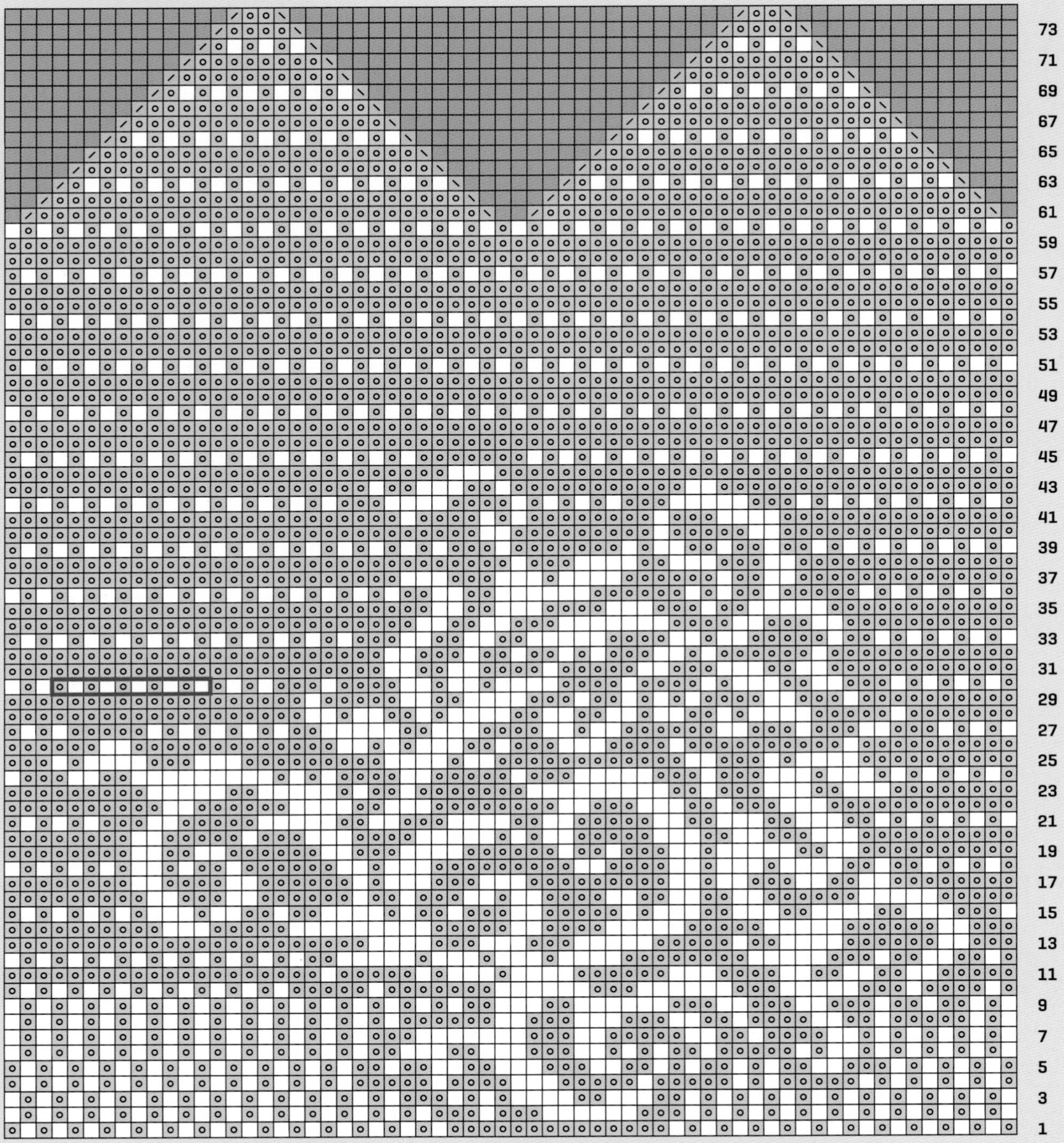

- with A, knit
- with B, knit
- with A, k2tog
- with A, ssk
- no stitch
- thumb placement

Right Mitten Chart

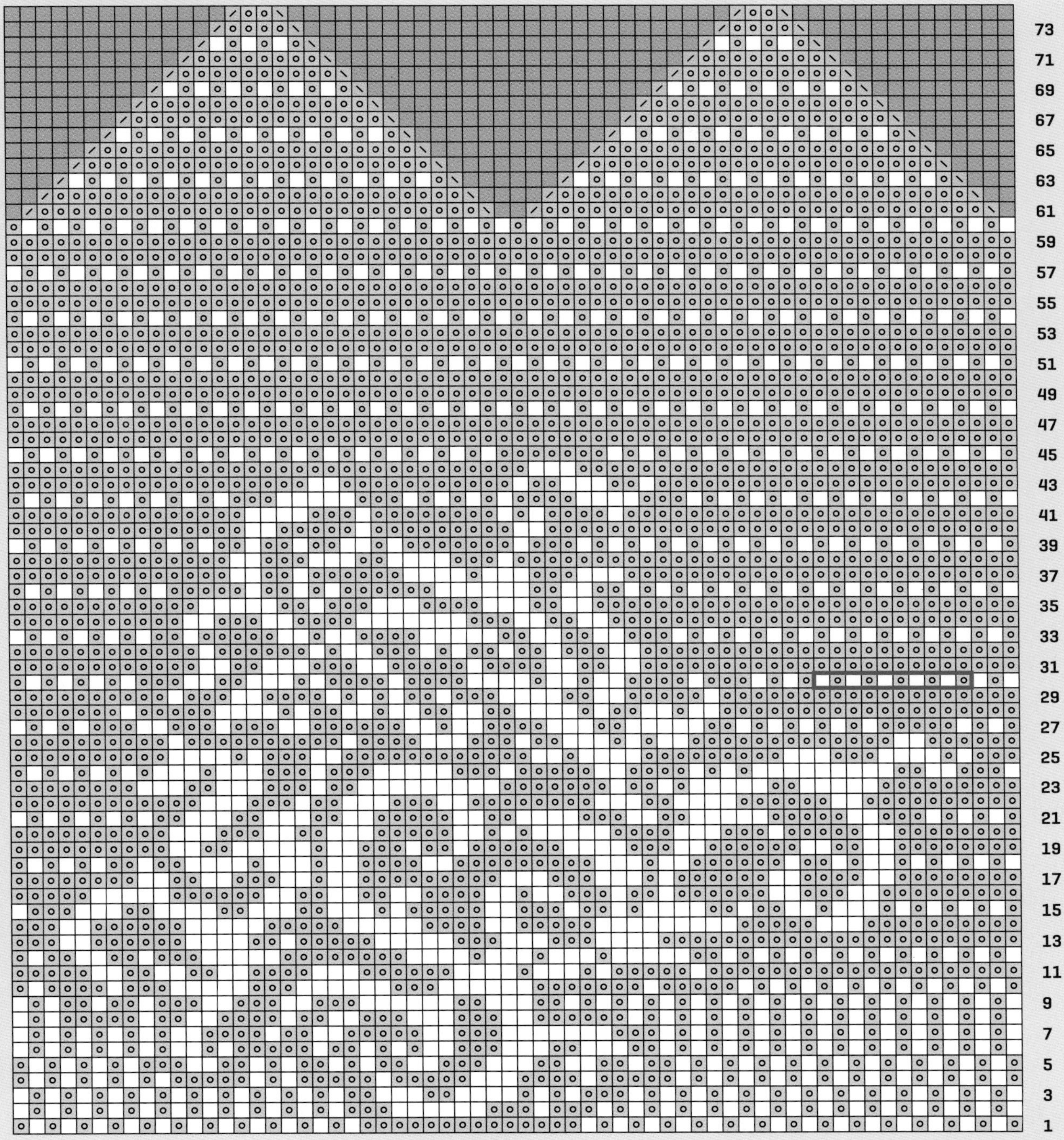

the *materials*

The materials an architect chooses can define a building. In selecting them, many factors come into play. Where is the structure located? Is the building being integrated into the landscape, and should (and can) indigenous materials be used? Is it on a fault line, and what is the climate? Can the outer materials withstand intense temperature shifts? What is the purpose of the building, and what are the existing structures in the surrounding area like? Is the idea to blend in, or to stand out?

As knitters, we choose our materials just as carefully. Do we want the drape of a loosely knit wool or bamboo, or perhaps a tightly knit linen or cotton?

What kind of needles do we use, and how tightly or loosely do the stitches need to be to get the proper fabric? Are we integrating a nontraditional material in with our yarn such as beads, wiring, or fabric? We, too, are building a structure, and determining the correct materials can mean the difference between ingenuity and failure in a garment.

In this chapter, you will see stunning examples of how materials carefully selected for knitting, much like those used in the world's most renowned architecture, create an indelible personality and visual identity for the finished piece.

tower of pisa SHIFT
Veera Välimäki

Knit sideways in the three lower panels, Veera Välimäki's shift sports a uniquely eye-catching construction that is joined as you go—not unlike how builders lay one columned story on top of the last. Made from an interesting combination of a silk and merino blend yarn held together with a soft stainless steel and silk yarn that can be worn against the skin, the shift gently molds to the wearer's form.

Finished size

30 (34¼, 38, 42¼, 46, 50¼)" (76 [87, 96.5, 107.5, 117, 127.5] cm) bust circumference.

Dress shown measures 34¼" (87 cm).

Yarn

Lace weight (#0 extra fine).

Shown here: SweetGeorgia Yarns, Merino Silk Lace (50% cultivated silk, 50% fine merino wool; 765 yd [700 m]/100 g): tumbled stone, 2 (2, 2, 2, 3, 3) skeins.

Habu Textiles, A-21 (69% silk, 31% metallic; 311 yds [284m]/14g): #3 gray, 1 (1, 1, 1, 1, 1) cone.

Needles

Size U.S. 4 (3.5 mm): two 24" (60 cm) circular (cir) and set of 2 double-pointed (dpn).

Adjust needle sizes if necessary to obtain the correct gauge.

Notions

Markers (m); stitch holders or waste yarn; tapestry needle; waste yarn for provisional CO.

Gauge

19 sts and 50 rows = 4" (10 cm) in Gtr st with 1 strand of each yarn held together (see Notes).

22 sts and 30 rows = 4" (10 cm) in St st with 1 strand of each yarn held together.

Notes: Garter st row gauge is important for the proper fit of this garment. The RS and WS of the lower body strips look very similar; it is recommended to place a removable marker or piece of waste yarn into the fabric on the RS to easily tell the difference. The lower body is worked sideways in three strips, joining together as they are knit. The upper body sts are picked up from the selvedge edge of the top strip and knit in the rnd.

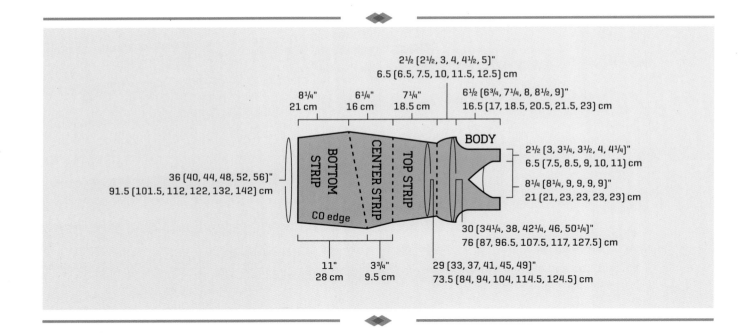

Bottom Strip

With waste yarn and cir needle, use a provisional method (see Techniques) to CO 66 sts. Do not join; work back and forth in rows.

With 1 strand of each yarn held together, knit 37 (41, 45, 49, 53, 57) rows.

Shape with short rows as foll

(**Note:** *Do not pick up wraps.*)

SHORT ROW 1: (RS) K20, w&t (see Techniques).

SHORT ROW 2: (WS) Knit to end.

SHORT ROW 3: K40, w&t.

SHORT ROW 4: Knit to end.

Decrease Section

*__DEC ROW:__ (RS) K2, ssk, knit to end—1 st dec'd.

NEXT ROW: Knit.

Rep the last 2 rows 3 more times—62 sts rem.

Knit 28 (32, 36, 40, 44, 48) rows, ending with a WS row.

Rep Short Rows 1–4.

Rep from * 3 more times—50 sts rem.

Piece should meas about 18 (20, 22, 24, 26, 28)" [45.5 (51, 56, 61, 66, 71) cm] to here along the shorter selvedge edge.

Knit 36 (40, 44, 48, 52, 56) rows, ending with a WS row.

Rep Short Rows 1–4.

Increase Section

**INC ROW: (RS) K2, M1 (see Techniques), knit to end—1 st inc'd.

NEXT ROW: Knit.

Rep the last 2 rows 3 more times—54 sts.

Knit 28 (32, 36, 40, 44, 48) rows, ending with a WS row.

Rep Short Rows 1–4.

Rep from ** 3 more times, ending after Short Row 3 of the last rep—66 sts.

Piece should meas about 36 (40, 44, 47, 52, 56)"

91.5 (101.5, 112, 122, 132, 142) cm to here along the shorter selvedge edge.

Carefully remove waste yarn from provisional sts and place 66 sts onto empty needle. With WS's held together, join sts using the three-needle BO method (see Techniques). Do not break yarn—400 (440, 480, 520, 560, 600) rows along the longer selvedge edge and 360 (400, 440, 480, 520, 560) rows along the shorter selvedge edge. Cont working center strip, picking up sts along the longer selvedge edge of the bottom strip as foll:

Center Strip

Use waste yarn and 1 strand of each working yarn held together, use the provisional method to CO 22 sts. Do not join; work back and forth in rows.

Cont working with 1 strand of each working yarn held together, picking up sts from the ends of bottom strip rows as foll:

NEXT ROW: (RS) Knit to end, pick up and knit 1 st from end of next bottom strip row and pass the last st over the picked up st.

NEXT ROW: (WS) Knit.

Rep the last 2 rows 17 (19, 21, 23, 25, 27) more times, then work 1 more RS row as est.

Shape with short rows as foll
(*Note:* Do not pick up wraps.)

SHORT ROW 5: (WS) K8, w&t.

SHORT ROW 6: (RS) Knit to end, pick up and knit 1 st from end of next bottom strip row and pass the last st over the picked up st.

SHORT ROW 7: K16, w&t.

SHORT ROW 8: Knit to end, pick up and knit 1 st from end of next bottom strip row and pass the last st over the picked up st.

Increase Section
*NEXT ROW: (WS) Knit.

INC ROW: (RS) K2, M1, knit to end, pick up and knit 1 st from end of next bottom strip row and pass the last st over the picked up st—1 st inc'd.

Rep the last 2 rows 3 more times—26 sts.

NEXT ROW: (WS) Knit.

NEXT ROW: (RS) Knit to end, pick up and knit 1 st from end of next bottom strip row and pass the last st over the picked up st.

Rep the last 2 rows 13 (15, 17, 19, 21, 23) more times.

Rep Short Rows 5–8.

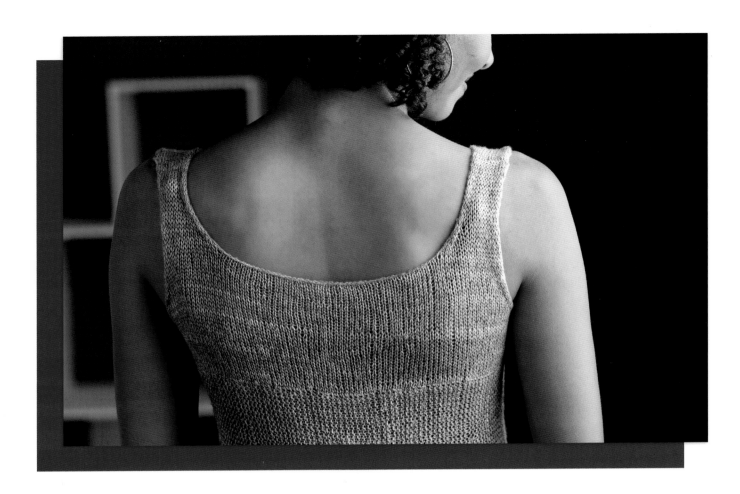

Rep from * 3 more times—38 sts.

NEXT ROW: (WS) Knit.

NEXT ROW: (RS) Knit to end, pick up and knit 1 st from end of next bottom strip row and pass the last st over the picked up st.

Rep the last 2 rows 17 (19, 21, 23, 25, 27) more times.

Rep Short Rows 5–8.

Decrease Section

**NEXT ROW: (WS) Knit.

DEC ROW: (RS) K2, ssk, knit to end, pick up and knit 1 st from end of next bottom strip row and pass the last st over the picked up st—1 st dec'd.

Rep the last 2 rows 3 more times—34 sts rem.

NEXT ROW: (WS) Knit.

NEXT ROW: (RS) Knit to end, pick up and knit 1 st from end of next bottom strip row and pass the last st over the picked up st.

Rep the last 2 rows 13 (15, 17, 19, 21, 23) more times.

Rep Short Rows 5–8.

Rep from ** 3 more times—22 sts rem.

Carefully remove waste yarn from provisional sts and place 22 sts onto empty needle. With WS's held together, join sts using the three-needle BO method. Do not break yarn—401 (441, 481, 521, 561, 601) rows along the longer pick-up edge and 361 (401, 441, 481, 521, 561) rows along the shorter selvedge edge. Cont working top strip, picking up sts along the shorter selvedge edge of the center strip as foll:

Top Strip

Using waste yarn and 1 strand of each working yarn held together, use a provisional method to CO 44 sts. Do not join; work back and forth in rows.

Cont working with 1 strand of each working yarn held together, picking up sts from the ends of the center strip rows as foll:

*NEXT ROW: (RS) Knit to end, pick up and knit 1 st from end of next center strip row and pass the last st over the picked up st.

NEXT ROW: (WS) Knit.

Rep the last 2 rows 14 (16, 18, 20, 22, 24) more times, then work 1 more RS row as est.

Shape with short rows as foll:

(**Note:** Do not pick up wraps.)

SHORT ROW 9: (WS) K10, w&t.

SHORT ROW 10: (RS) Knit to end, pick up and knit 1 st from end of next bottom strip row and pass the last st over the picked up st.

SHORT ROW 11: K20, w&t.

SHORT ROW 12: Knit to end, pick up and knit 1 st from end of next bottom strip row and pass the last st over the picked up st.

SHORT ROW 13: K30, w&t.

SHORT ROW 14: Knit to end, pick up and knit 1 st from end of next bottom strip row and pass the last st over the picked up st.

NEXT ROW: (WS) Knit.

Rep from * 9 more times.

NEXT ROW: (RS) Knit.

Carefully remove waste yarn from provisional sts and place 44 sts onto empty needle. With WS held together, join sts using the three-needle BO method. Do not break yarn—361 (401, 441, 481, 521, 561) rows along the longer pick-up edge and 291 (331, 371, 411, 451, 491) rows along the shorter selvedge edge.

Upper Body

Lay piece flat so three-needle BO is at one edge, place a removable marker at the other edge to mark side. Cont working body, picking up sts along the shorter selvedge edge of the top strip as foll:

Pm for beg of rnd and cont working with yarn attached to top strip, there is 1 st on right needle, pick up and knit 81 (93, 103, 115, 125, 137) more sts to m for front, remove m from fabric and place onto needle for side, pick up and knit 83 (93, 105, 115, 127, 137) sts to end for back. Join to work in the rnd—165 (189, 209, 233, 253, 277) sts.

Work in St st until piece meas 2½ (2½, 3, 4, 4½, 5)" (6.5 [6.5, 7.5, 10, 11.5, 12.5] cm) from pick-up rnd, ending last rnd 2 (4, 5, 6, 6, 10) sts before beg of rnd m.

Divide for Back and Fronts

BO 4 (8, 10, 12, 12, 20) sts, knit to 2 (4, 5, 6, 6, 10) sts before side m, BO 4 (8, 10, 12, 12, 20) sts, knit to end—79 (87, 95, 105, 115, 119) sts rem on needle for back. Cont working back and forth on back sts only. Divide front sts into 2 equal halves and place them on separate st holders or waste yarn—39 (43, 47, 52, 57, 59) sts rem each front.

Back
Shape Armholes

NEXT ROW: (WS) Purl.

DEC ROW: (RS) K3, ssk, work to last 5 sts, k2tog, k3—2 sts dec'd.

Rep the last 2 rows 2 (3, 4, 7, 10, 10) more times—73 (79, 85, 89, 93, 97) sts rem.

Cont working in St st until armholes meas 2 (2, 2, 2½, 3, 3½)" (5 [5, 5, 6.5, 7.5, 9] cm) from divide, ending with a WS row.

Get Inspired

Built in the early Twelfth century over the course of 344 years, the Tower of Pisa stands eight stories high, originally housed seven bells (which were later removed to alleviate weight), and—after much reconstruction and stabilizing—leans at an almost four-degree angle. Built in three major phases, the tower began to lean to one side during the second phase of construction because of its placement on weak ground. During its most recent stabilization in 2008, engineers determined it would not deepen its tilt for the next two hundred years.

Shape Neck

NEXT ROW: (RS) K17 (19, 21, 23, 25, 27), pm, k39 (41, 43, 43, 43, 43), then place these sts onto st holder or waste yarn, remove m, knit to end—17 (19, 21, 23, 25, 27) sts rem on each side. Cont working left back sts only, keeping right back sts on needle to be worked later.

Left Back Shoulder

NEXT ROW: (WS) Purl to neck edge.

DEC ROW: (RS) K2, ssk, knit to end—1 st dec'd.

Rep the last 2 rows 2 more times—14 (16, 18, 20, 22, 24) sts rem.

Cont working in St st until armhole meas 6½ (6¾, 7¼, 8, 8½, 9)" (16.5 [17, 18.5, 20.5, 21.5, 23] cm) from divide. Place sts onto st holder or waste yarn. Break yarn and set aside.

Right Back Shoulder

Rejoin 1 strand of each working yarn to the 17 (19, 21, 23, 25, 27) right shoulder sts, preparing to work a WS row.

NEXT ROW: (WS) Purl.

DEC ROW: (RS) Knit to last 4 sts, k2tog, k2—14 (16, 18, 20, 22, 24) sts rem.

Cont working in St st until armhole meas 6½ (6¾, 7¼, 8, 8½, 9)" (16.5 [17, 18.5, 20.5, 21.5, 23] cm) from divide. Place sts on st holder or waste yarn. Break yarn and set aside.

Left Front

Return 39 (43, 47, 52, 57, 59) held left front sts onto cir needle and rejoin 1 strand of each yarn, preparing to work a WS row.

Shape Armhole and Neck

NEXT ROW: (WS) Purl.

DEC ROW: (RS) K3, ssk, knit to last 4 sts, k2tog, k2—2 sts dec'd.

Rep the last 2 rows 2 (3, 4, 7, 10, 10) more times—33 (35, 37, 36, 35, 37) sts rem.

Shape Neck

NEXT ROW: (WS) Purl.

DEC ROW: (RS) Knit to last 4 sts, k2tog, k2—1 st dec'd.

Rep the last 2 rows 18 (18, 18, 15, 12, 12) more times—14 (16, 18, 20, 22, 24) sts rem.

Cont working in St st until armhole meas 6½ (6¾, 7¼, 8, 8½, 9)" (16.5 [17, 18.5, 20.5, 21.5, 23] cm) from divide.

Join Left Shoulder

Sl rem sts onto dpn. Return held left back sts onto a second dpn and join with front sts using the three-needle BO.

Right Front

Return 39 (44, 47, 52, 57, 60) held right front sts onto cir needle and rejoin 1 strand of each yarn preparing to work a WS row.

Shape Armhole and Neck

NEXT ROW: (WS) Purl.

DEC ROW: (RS) K2, ssk, knit to last 5 sts, k2tog, k3—2 sts dec'd.

Rep the last 2 rows 2 (3, 4, 7, 10, 10) more times—33 (35, 37, 36, 35, 37) sts rem.

Shape Neck

NEXT ROW: (WS) Purl.

DEC ROW: (RS) K2, ssk, knit to end—1 st dec'd.

Rep the last 2 rows 18 (18, 18, 15, 12, 12) more times—14 (16, 18, 20, 22, 24) sts rem.

Cont working in St st until armhole meas 6½ (6¾, 7¼, 8, 8½, 9)" (16.5 [17, 18.5, 20.5, 21.5, 23] cm) from divide.

Join Right Shoulder

Sl rem sts onto dpn. Return held right back sts onto a second dpn and join with front sts using the three-needle BO.

Finishing

Weave in all loose ends. Block the dress to measurements.

bauhaus CARDIGAN
Ann Weaver

Worked in one piece from the bottom up to the armholes, Ann Weaver's Bauhaus-inspired cardigan joins a merino, alpaca, and silk blend yarn with intarsia mohair accents to give this wardrobe classic a textured look. Straightforward shaping, stockinette stitch, short rows, a garter stitch collar, and button bands emphasize the idea taught at the famous school that less is more.

Finished measurements

About 35¾ (40¼, 43¾, 48¼, 51)" (91 [102, 111, 122.5, 131.5] cm) bust circumference with 1" (2.5 cm) front overlap.

Cardigan shown measures 35¾" (91 cm) and is designed to fit with no ease, but the fabric has a good deal of stretch and the shoulders and upper arms are loose for easy layering.

Yarn

DK weight (#3 Light).

Shown here: The Fibre Company Acadia (60% merino wool, 20% baby alpaca, 20% silk; 145 yd [133 m]/50 g): driftwood (A), 9 (10, 11, 12, 13) skeins.

Lace weight (#0 lace).

Shown here: Be Sweet Extra Fine Mohair (100% baby mohair; 230 yd [210 m]/25 g): #35b dark blue plum (B); #10 tobacco (C); #18 pale green (D), 1 skein each.

Needles

Body: Sizes U.S. 5 and 6 (3.75 and 4 mm): 32" (80 cm) circular (cir).

Sleeves: Sizes U.S. 5 and 6 (3.75 and 4 mm): double-pointed (dpn).

Collar: Size U.S. 4 (3.5 mm): 16" (40.5 cm) cir.

Adjust needle sizes if necessary to obtain the correct gauge.

Notions

Markers (m); stitch holders or waste yarn; 14 (14, 14, 15, 15) ⅝" (1.5 cm) buttons; tapestry needle.

Gauge

22 sts and 28 rows = 4" (10 cm) in St st with largest needles.

Notes: The body is worked in one piece to the underarms. The sleeves are worked in the round to the underarms, where they are joined to the body. From this point on, the cardigan is worked in one piece to the end.

Body

Using medium cir and A, CO 186 (206, 226, 246, 266) sts. Do not join; work back and forth in rows.

Work in St st until piece meas 1" (2.5 cm) from beg, ending with a WS row.

TURNING ROW: (RS) Change to largest cir and purl.

Cont working even in St st until piece meas 1" (2.5 cm) from turning row, ending with a WS row.

JOIN HEM: (RS) Fold piece along turning row, holding WS's together, and hold CO edge directly behind sts on needle, *insert tip of left needle into st of CO edge that is directly behind first st on needle, knit this st together with first st on needle; rep from * until all sts have been worked.

Cont working even in St st until piece meas 3" (7.5 cm) from turning row, ending with a WS row.

(*Note: Read the foll instructions carefully before beg: Intarsia and buttonholes beg at the same time, and waist shaping beg before they are finished.*)

BUTTONHOLE ROW: (RS) K3, yo, k2tog, work to end as est.

Work 11 rows as est, ending with a WS row.

Rep the last 12 rows 13 (13, 13, 14, 14) more times, then work buttonhole row once more; *at the same time*, on first buttonhole row, beg intarsia as foll:

EST INTARSIA: (RS) With A: k48 (53, 58, 63, 68), pm for side, k30 (35, 40, 45, 50), pm for intarsia, join B, k30, pm for intarsia, join a second ball of A, k30 (35, 40, 45, 50), pm for side, k48 (53, 58, 63, 68) to end.

Work as est for 6" (15 cm), ending with a WS row. Break B and the ball of A at the middle of the row.

With A: work in St st for 8 rows, ending with a WS row.

NEXT ROW: (RS) With A: knit to first intarsia m, sl m, join C, k30, sl m, join a second ball of A and knit to end.

Work as est for 6" (15 cm), ending with a WS row. Break C and the ball of A at the middle of the row.

With A: work in St st for 8 rows, ending with a WS row.

NEXT ROW: (RS) With A: knit to first intarsia m, sl m, join D, k30, sl m, join a second ball of A and knit to end.

Work as est for 6" (15 cm), ending with a WS row. Break D and the ball of A at the middle of the row.

Cont with A for remainder of piece; *at the same time*, when piece meas 6 (6, 6, 6½, 6½)" (15 [15, 15, 16.5, 16.5] cm) from turning row, end with a WS row.

Shape Waist

DEC ROW: (RS) Knit to 2 sts before side m, ssk, sl m, k1, k2tog, work as est to 3 sts before next side m, ssk, k1, sl m, k2tog, knit to end—4 sts dec'd.

Work 11 rows even.

Rep the last 12 rows once more—178 (198, 218, 238, 258) sts rem.

Work 8 rows even, ending with a WS row.

INC ROW: (RS) Knit to side m, M1, sl m, k1, M1, work to 1 st before next side m, M1, k1, sl m, M1, knit to end—4 sts inc'd.

Work 11 rows straight.

Rep previous 12 rows once more—186 (206, 226, 246, 266) sts.

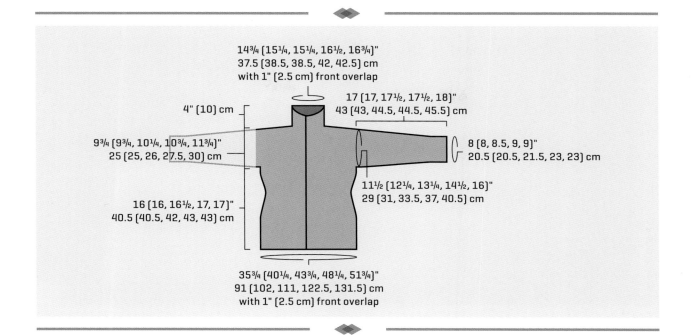

14¾ [15¼, 15¼, 16½, 16¾]"
37.5 [38.5, 38.5, 42, 42.5] cm
with 1" [2.5 cm] front overlap

4" [10] cm

17 [17, 17½, 17½, 18]"
43 [43, 44.5, 44.5, 45.5] cm

9¾ [9¾, 10¼, 10¾, 11¾]"
25 [25, 26, 27.5, 30] cm

8 [8, 8.5, 9, 9]"
20.5 [20.5, 21.5, 23, 23] cm

11½ [12¼, 13¼, 14½, 16]"
29 [31, 33.5, 37, 40.5] cm

16 [16, 16½, 17, 17]"
40.5 [40.5, 42, 43, 43] cm

35¾ [40¼, 43¾, 48¼, 51¾]"
91 [102, 111, 122.5, 131.5] cm
with 1" [2.5 cm] front overlap

Work even as est until piece meas 16 (16, 16½, 17, 17)" (40.5 [40.5, 42, 43, 43] cm) from turning row, ending with a RS row.

DIVIDE FOR BACK AND FRONT: (WS) Purl to 5 (5, 5, 6, 6) sts before side m, BO next 10 (10, 10, 12, 12) sts, purl to 5 (5, 5, 6, 6) sts before next side m, BO next 10 (10, 10, 12, 12) sts, purl to end—43 (48, 53, 57, 62) sts for each front, 80 (90, 100, 108, 118) sts for back.

Keep sts on needle. Do not break yarn, and set aside.

Sleeve [make 2]

With smaller dpn and A, CO 45 (45, 47, 50, 50) sts. Join to work in the rnd, being careful not to twist sts. Pm to indicate beg of rnd.

Work even in St st until piece meas 1" (2.5 cm) from beg.

TURNING RND: Change to larger dpn and purl.

Cont working in St st until piece meas 1" (2.5 cm) from turning row.

JOIN HEM: Fold piece along turning rnd, holding WS together, and hold CO edge directly behind sts on

needle, *insert tip of left needle into st of CO edge that is directly behind first st on needle, knit this st together with first st on needle; rep from * until all sts have been worked.

Cont working even in St st until piece meas 4 (4, 4, 3, 3)" (10 [10, 10, 7.5, 7.5] cm) from turning rnd.

Shape Sleeve

INC RND: K1, M1, knit to last st, M1, k1—2 sts inc'd.

Work 9 (7, 6, 5, 4) rnds even.

Rep the last 10 (8, 7, 6, 5) rnds 8 (10, 12, 14, 18) more times—63 (67, 73, 80, 88) sts.

Cont working in St st until piece meas 17 (17, 17½, 17½, 18)" (43 [43, 44.5, 44.5, 45.5] cm) from turning rnd, ending last rnd 5 (5, 5, 6, 6) sts before beg of rnd m.

DIVIDE FOR UNDERARM: BO 10 (10, 10, 12, 12) sts, knit to end—53 (57, 63, 68, 76) sts.

Place rem sts onto st holder or waste yarn. Break yarn and set aside.

Make second sleeve the same as the first.

Yoke

Cont working with needle and yarn from body as foll:

JOINING ROW: (RS) K43 (48, 53, 57, 62) right front sts, place 53 (57, 63, 68, 76) sts from 1 sleeve onto left needle and knit across, pm, k80 (90, 100, 108, 118) back sts, pm, place 53 (57, 63, 68, 76) sts from second sleeve onto left needle and knit across, k43 (48, 53, 57, 62) left front sts—272 (300, 332, 358, 394) sts.

Cont working as est until yoke meas 5 (5, 5, 5½, 5½)" (12.5 [12.5, 12.5, 14, 14] cm) from joining row, ending with a WS row.

Shape Yoke

DEC ROW 1: (RS) [K1, k2tog] 31 (35, 38, 41, 46) times, k3 (0, 2, 2, 0), sl m, [k2tog] 11 (15, 17, 19, 22) times, k1 (0, 1, 1, 0), sl m, k15 sts of Intarsia Panel, pm, knit to end of Intarsia Panel, sl m, k1 (0, 1, 1, 0), [ssk] 11 (15, 17, 19, 22) times, sl m, k3 (0, 2, 2, 0), [ssk, k1] 31 (35, 38, 41, 46) times—188 (200, 222, 238, 258) sts.

Cont working as est until yoke meas 7½ (7½, 7½, 8, 8½)" (19 [19, 19, 20.5, 21.5] cm) from joining row, ending with a WS row.

*(**Note:** By this point, intarsia blocks are completed. Remove markers, keeping only the m placed at the center of the Intarsia Panel on Dec Rnd 1.)*

DEC ROW 2: (RS) [K1, k2tog] 31 (33, 36, 39, 43) times, k1 (1, 3, 2, 0), sl m, k1 (1, 3, 2, 0), [ssk, k1] 31 (33, 36, 39, 43) times—126 (134, 150, 160, 172) sts.

Work as established until yoke meas 9 (9, 9½, 10, 10½)" (23 [23, 24, 25.5, 26.5] cm) from joining row, ending with a WS row.

Cont for your size as foll:

Sizes 35¾ [40¼]" only:
DEC ROW 3: (RS) [K1, k2tog] 20 (22) times, k3 (1), sl m, k3 (1), [ssk, k1] 20 (22) times—86 (90) sts.

Sizes 43¾ [48¼, 51¾]" only:
DEC ROW 3: (RS) [K1, k2tog, k2tog] 15 (16, 17) times, k0 (0, 1), sl m, k0 (0, 1), [ssk, ssk, k1] 15 (16, 17) times—90 (96, 104) sts.

All sizes:
Work 3 rows even in St st, ending with a WS row.

Size 51¾" only:
DEC ROW 4: (RS) K14, [k2tog, k13] 6 times—98 sts rem.

Work 3 rows even in St st, ending with a WS row.

Neck Shaping

All sizes:

(*Note:* *If a buttonhole rem to be worked, work it on the following RS row.*)

Work short rows to shape the back of the neck:

ROW 1: (RS) Knit to 12 (12, 12, 14, 16) sts after m, w&t (see Techniques).

ROW 2: (WS) Purl to 12 (12, 12, 14, 16) sts after m, w&t.

ROW 3: (RS) Knit to wrapped st, knit next st together with the wrap, k4, w&t.

ROW 4: (WS) Purl to wrapped st, purl next st together with the wrap, p4, w&t.

ROW 5: (RS) Knit to end, knitting wrap together with the wrapped st.

ROW 6: (WS) Purl to end, purling wrap together with the wrapped st.

Collar

Change to smallest cir and work in Gtr st for 4" (10 cm), ending with a RS row. BO all sts kwise on WS row.

Finishing

Block piece to measurements. Sew underarms.

Right Front Edging

With RS facing, beg at lower right front edge, use A and largest cir to pick up and knit 157 (157, 162, 167, 173) sts evenly along right front and collar edge. Knit 4 rows, ending with a RS row. BO all sts kwise on WS row.

Left Front Edging

With RS facing, beg at left front collar edge, use A and largest cir to pick up and knit 157 (157, 162, 167, 173) sts evenly along right front and collar edge. Knit 4 rows, ending with a RS row. BO all sts kwise on WS row.

Sew buttons to body opposite buttonholes.

Get Inspired

A driving force behind modernism, the Bauhaus movement was started by German architect Walter Gropius in 1919. With a focus on simplicity and function, students of the Bauhaus school believed that all art forms should work together to create a new philosophy in design. Moving among three German cities and as a result continually shifting its focus, the school closed its doors in 1933 due to Nazi pressure.

hotel tassel WRAP
Åsa Tricosa

Wearing Åsa Tricosa's stunning lace and cabled wrap is like wrapping yourself in a work of fine art. Molding the yarn into an Art Nouveau–inspired mix of lace mesh, garter edge detail, and a cabled motif that runs its full length, this wrap shows as much thought in every stitch as Victor Horta put into his masterpiece, Hotel Tassel.

Finished measurements
About 19" (48.5 cm) wide × 58" (147.5 cm) long.

Yarn
Lace weight (#0 lace).

Shown here: Miss Babs Yet (65% merino, 35% tussah silk; 400 yd [366 m]/65 g): moss, 2 skeins.

Needles
Wrap: Size U.S. 4 (3.5 mm): 32" (80 cm) circular (cir).

Cast-On: Size U.S. 3 (3.25 mm): 32" (80 cm) cir.

Adjust needle sizes if necessary to obtain the correct gauge.

Notions
Two cable needles (cn); stitch holder or waste yarn; tapestry needle.

Gauge
19 sts and 32 rows = 4" (10 cm) in Mesh pattern with larger needle.

Notes: When working only part of the sts on a cn, work the sts on the right on the cn and keep the st(s) on the left on the cn to be worked later.

Stitch Guide

Mesh Pattern

(multiple of 3 sts + 2)

(Note: This pattern as written here is only used for the gauge swatch. This patt is incorporated into Charts A and B.)

ROW 1: (RS) K1, *k2tog, yo, k1; rep from * to last st, k1.

ROWS 2 AND 4: (WS) Purl.

ROW 3: K2, *k2tog, yo, k1; rep from *.

ROW 5: K1, *yo, k1, k2tog; rep from * to last st, k1.

ROW 6: Purl.

Rep Rows 1–6 for patt.

Attached I-Cord Edging

Use the cable method (see Techniques) to CO 3 sts, k4, *sl 4 sts from right needle to left needle, k3, k2togtbl; rep from * until 4 sts rem on right needle, sl 4 sts from right needle to left needle, sl 1, BO 1, k2togtbl, pass slipped st over—1 st rem. Fasten off.

Mesh Chart
(used for gauge swatch only)

/	o	
o	/	
	o	/

Rows: 5, 3, 1

☐ knit on RS, purl on WS

▣ yo

⊡ k2tog

☐ pattern repeat

Wrap

With smaller cir needle, use the Turkish method (see Techniques) to CO 109 sts.

Change to larger needle.

SET-UP ROW: (WS) Sl 1 pwise wyf, k1, sl 1 pwise wyf, purl to last 3 sts, sl 1 pwise wyf, k1, sl 1 pwise wyf. Sl sts from provisional CO onto st holder or waste yarn.

Work Rows 1–100 of Chart A—*103 sts rem.*

Work Rows 101–106 forty-five times.

Work Rows 1–98 of Chart B—*109 sts.*

BO using the attached I-cord edging (see Stitch Guide).

Finishing

Carefully remove waste yarn from provisional CO and return 109 sts to larger cir needle. BO using the attached I-cord edging.

Weave in loose ends. Block to measurements.

Get Inspired

Designed by the famous Art Nouveau architect Victor Horta, Belgium's Hotel Tassel is one of the most recognized buildings from that era. The structure consists of two main buildings built with brick and stone, joined together by a third glass-covered steel building, bringing light into the center. This building is unique because each element was designed by Horta himself, from the doorknobs, to the staircases, to the mosaic-covered flooring, to the wall panels down to the windows.

Chart A

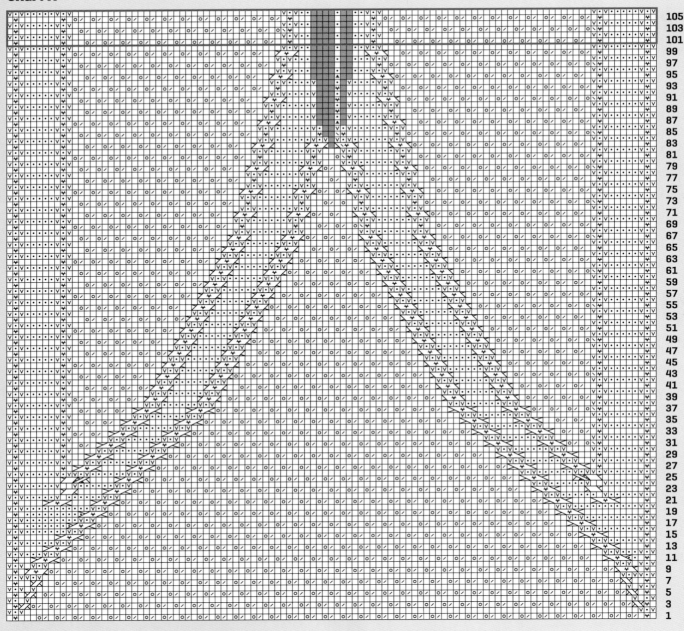

105
103
101
99
97
95
93
91
89
87
85
83
81
79
77
75
73
71
69
67
65
63
61
59
57
55
53
51
49
47
45
43
41
39
37
35
33
31
29
27
25
23
21
19
17
15
13
11
9
7
5
3
1

☐	knit on RS, purl on WS	Ⓡ	M1R
•	purl on RS, knit on WS	Ⓛ	M1L
◯	yo	Ⓟ	M1P
╱	k2tog	⊞	kfb
╲	ssk	☐	pattern repeat
⊻	sl 1 pwise wyf on RS	✕	sl 1 st onto cn and hold in front, k1, k1 from cn
⋁	sl 1 pwise wyf on WS	✕	sl 1 st onto cn and hold in back, k1, k1 from cn
⋀	s2kp	✕	sl 3 sts onto cn and hold in front, k1; k1, sl 1 pwise wyf, k1 from cn
▣	no stitch		

Chart B

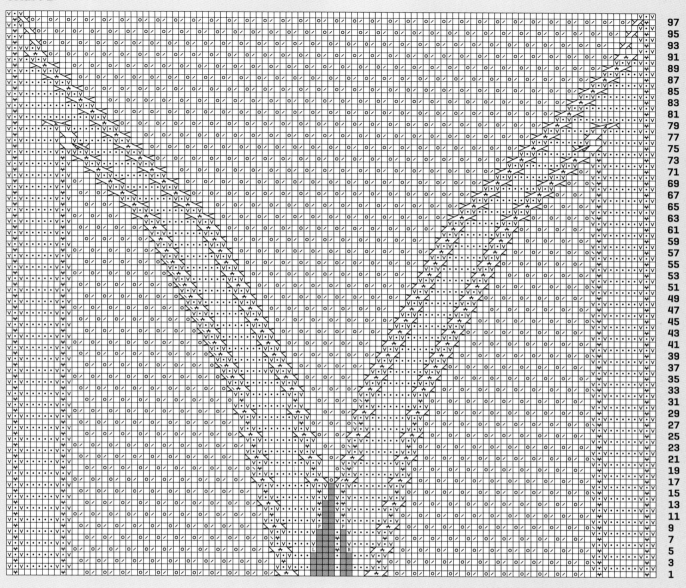

97
95
93
91
89
87
85
83
81
79
77
75
73
71
69
67
65
63
61
59
57
55
53
51
49
47
45
43
41
39
37
35
33
31
29
27
25
23
21
19
17
15
13
11
9
7
5
3
1

sl 1 st onto cn and hold in back, k1, sl 1 pwise wyf, k1; k1 from cn

sl 2 sts onto cn and hold in back, k1, sl 1 pwise wyf, k1; k2 from cn

sl 3 sts onto cn and hold in front, k2; k1, sl 1 pwise wyf, k1 from cn

sl 2 sts onto cn and hold in front, k1; k2 from cn

sl 1 st onto cn and hold in back, k2; k1 from cn

sl 3 sts onto cn and hold in front, k1 from left needle; k2 from cn; k1 from left needle; k1 from cn

sl 2 sts onto cn and hold in back, k1 from left needle; k1 from cn; k2 from left needle; k1 from cn

sl 3 sts onto cn and hold in front, k1; k1, sl 1 pwise wyf from cn, ssk last st of cn with next st on left needle

sl 1 st onto cn and hold in back, k2 from left needle, sl 1 st onto second cn and hold in back, k1 from left needle, k1 from first cn, k1 from second cn

sl 1 st onto cn and hold in front, k1 from left needle, sl 2 sts onto second cn and hold in front, k1 from left needle, k1 from first cn, k2 from second cn

sl 3 sts onto cn and hold in front, [kfb] 2 times, sk2p from cn

sl 2 sts onto cn and hold in back, k3tog, [kfb] 2 times from cn

Bird's Nest SHRUG
Tanis Gray

Worked sideways, then partially seamed to create sleeves, Tanis Gray's architectural beaded shrug is a medley of texture and glamour. A horizontal rib and slip-stitch pattern has beads crocheted in to emphasize the cabling at a seemingly random interval, yet it is done very much in an orderly fashion. A lace collar knit separately and attached with a three-needle bind-off completes the structured look.

Finished measurements
17¼" (44 cm) wide × 23½" (59.5 cm) long, excluding collar.

Yarn
Worsted weight (#4 worsted).

Shown here: Neighborhood Fiber Co. Studio Worsted (100% superwash merino; 400 yd [366 m]/226 g): Logan Circle, 1 skein.

Needles
Shrug: Size U.S. 8 (5 mm): 24" (60 cm) circular (cir).

Bind-Off: Size U.S. 13 (9 mm): straight needle.

Adjust needle sizes if necessary to obtain the correct gauge.

Notions
Size U.S. 13 (0.75 mm) crochet hook; 540 size 6/0 Miyuki chartreuse beads; tapestry needle.

Gauge
18 sts and 32 rows = 4" (10 cm) in Bird's Nest pattern with smaller needle.

Stitch Guide

2×2 Ribbing
(multiple of 4 sts)

ROW 1: (WS) P1, *p2, k2; rep from * to last 3 sts, p3.

ROW 2: K3, *p2, k2; rep from * to last st, k1.

Rep Rows 1 and 2 for patt.

PB (place bead)
Place bead on crochet hook, drop st from left needle and draw it through the bead using the crochet hook, sl the st onto the right needle.

Sleeve

With smaller needle, CO 68 sts, leaving about 12" (30.5 cm) tail for seaming.

Work in 2×2 ribbing (see Stitch Guide) for 15 rows, ending with a WS row.

INC ROW: (RS) K7, *M1 (see Techniques), k6; rep from * to last st, k1—78 sts.

Body

Set-up for Bird's Nest chart as foll:

SET-UP ROW 1: (RS) Purl.

SET-UP ROW 2: Knit.

SET-UP ROW 3: Knit.

SET-UP ROW 4: P3, *p15, [PB] (see Stitch Guide) 2 times, p2, [PB] 2 times, p3; rep from * to last 3 sts, p3.

Work Rows 1–32 of Bird's Nest chart 4 times, then work Rows 1–15 once more.

Sleeve

DEC ROW: (WS) P7 *p2tog, p5; rep from * to last st, p1—68 sts rem.

Work in 2 × 2 ribbing for 15 rows, ending with a RS row.

BO all sts loosely kwise, leaving about 12" (30.5 cm) tail for seaming.

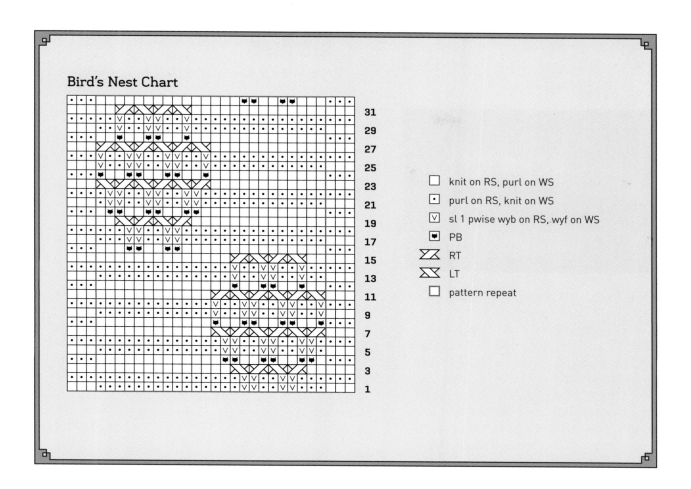

Bird's Nest Chart

☐	knit on RS, purl on WS	
·	purl on RS, knit on WS	
�	sl 1 pwise wyb on RS, wyf on WS	
⬛	PB	
⟋⟍	RT	
⟍⟋	LT	
☐	pattern repeat	

Row numbers shown: 1, 3, 5, 7, 9, 11, 13, 15, 17, 19, 21, 23, 25, 27, 29, 31

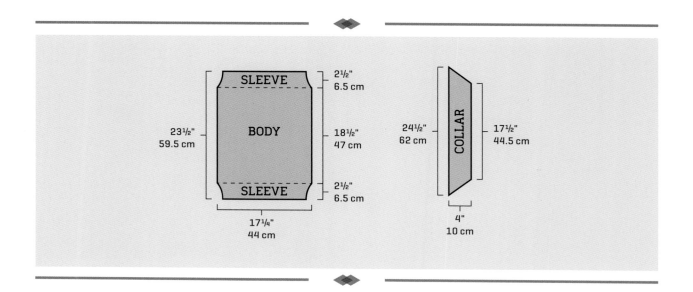

SLEEVE

2½"
6.5 cm

23½"
59.5 cm

BODY

18½"
47 cm

SLEEVE

2½"
6.5 cm

17¼"
44 cm

24½"
62 cm

COLLAR

17½"
44.5 cm

4"
10 cm

Collar

With smaller needle, CO 15 sts.

Work Rows 1–14 of Collar chart 14 times. BO all sts loosely.

Block lightly.

Finishing

Block lightly to measurements.

Use long tails to seam sleeves along ribbing for 2½" (6.5 cm).

JOIN COLLAR: With smaller needle and WS of body facing, pick up and knit 84 sts along 1 long edge between sleeves of body, then with RS of collar facing, pick up and knit 84 sts along flat selvedge edge of collar. With larger needle, RS of body facing and WS of collar (so when turned over, RS of collar shows), join pieces using the three-needle BO (see Techniques).

Weave in loose ends.

Get Inspired

Constructed as a point for the 2008 Summer Olympics and Paralympics in China, the Beijing National Stadium is commonly referred to as the "Bird's Nest." Inspired by ancient Chinese pottery, this engineering marvel with its 110,000-ton twisting mass of steel beams looks random but is intricately laid out to hide the inner structure. Designed in a bowl shape with a roof that curves in to shield occupants from inclement weather, an 80,000-person capacity, a cost of almost five hundred million dollars and much controversy, the Bird's Nest is considered one of the most iconic buildings of the twenty-first century thus far.

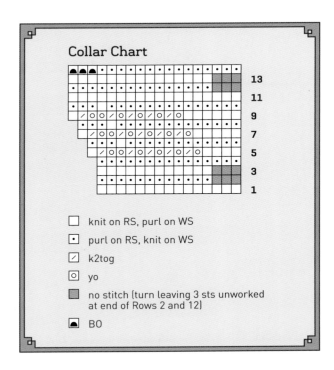

Collar Chart

☐ knit on RS, purl on WS

· purl on RS, knit on WS

╱ k2tog

○ yo

▨ no stitch (turn leaving 3 sts unworked at end of Rows 2 and 12)

◼ BO

erechtheion PULLOVER
Maria Leigh

In Maria Leigh's draped boatneck pullover, the front and back pieces are knit flat, then seamed. The sleeves are the star of the show—by picking up and knitting stitches at the armhole edge, then increasing out in a circular fashion, sleeves are created with a beautiful, dramatic drape that will look appealing on any figure. Support structures on many temples, created in the form of female figures, used drapery to flatter and contour the body, giving off a hint of sexuality and fertility.

Finished measurements
About 32 (36½, 40½, 45, 49, 53½" (81.5 [92.5, 103, 114.5, 124.5, 136] cm) bust circumference.

Pullover shown measures 36½" (92.5 cm).

Yarn
DK weight (#3 DK).

Shown here: Classic Elite Yarns Wool Bam Boo (50% wool, 50% bamboo viscose; 118 yd [108 m]/50 g): #1650 vanilla, 11 (12, 13, 14, 16, 17) skeins.

Needles
Size U.S. 6 (4 mm): 16" and 32" (40 and 80 cm) circular (cir) and set of 4 or 5 double-pointed (dpn).

Adjust needle size if necessary to obtain the correct gauge.

Notions
Markers (m); tapestry needle.

Gauge
21 sts and 28 rows = 4" (10 cm) in St st.

Back

With longer cir needle, CO 90 (102, 112, 124, 134, 146) sts. Do not join; work back and forth in rows.

Work in Gtr st until piece meas 1¼" (3.2 cm) from beg, ending with a WS row.

Work in St st until piece meas 2½" (6.5 cm) from beg, ending with a WS row.

Shape Waist

DEC ROW: (RS) K1, k2tog, knit to last 3 sts, ssk, k1—2 sts dec'd.

Work even in St st for 9 (7, 7, 7, 7, 7) rows, ending with a WS row.

Rep the last 10 (8, 8, 8, 8, 8) rows 5 (6, 6, 6, 6, 6) more times, then work dec row once more—76 (86, 96, 108, 118, 130) sts rem.

Cont working even in St st until piece meas 12¼ (12, 11¾, 11½, 11, 11)" (31 ([30.5, 30, 29, 28, 28] cm) from beg, ending with a WS row.

INC ROW: (RS) K2, M1L (see Techniques), knit to last 2 sts, M1R (see Techniques), k2—2 sts inc'd.

Work even in St st for 7 (5, 5, 5, 5, 5) rows, ending with a WS row.

Rep the last 8 (6, 6, 6, 6, 6) rows 3 (4, 4, 4, 4, 4) more times—84 (96, 106, 118, 128, 140) sts.

Cont working even in St st until piece meas 18¼ (18, 17¾, 17½, 17, 17)" (46.5 (45.5, 45, 44.5, 43, 43] cm) from beg, ending with a WS row.

Shape Armholes

BO 4 (5, 6, 8, 9, 10) sts at beg of next 2 rows, BO 3 sts at beg of next 0 (2, 2, 2, 4, 4) rows, then BO 2 sts at beg of next 2 (0, 2, 2, 0, 2) rows—72 (80, 84, 92, 98, 104) sts rem.

DEC ROW: (RS) K1, k2tog, knit to last 3 sts, ssk, k1—2 sts dec'd.

NEXT ROW: Purl.

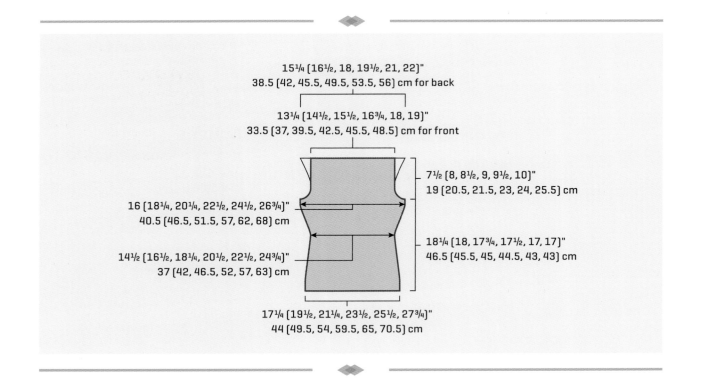

15¼ [16½, 18, 19½, 21, 22]"
38.5 [42, 45.5, 49.5, 53.5, 56] cm for back

13¼ [14½, 15½, 16¾, 18, 19]"
33.5 [37, 39.5, 42.5, 45.5, 48.5] cm for front

7½ [8, 8½, 9, 9½, 10]"
19 [20.5, 21.5, 23, 24, 25.5] cm

16 [18¼, 20¼, 22½, 24½, 26¾]"
40.5 [46.5, 51.5, 57, 62, 68] cm

18¼ [18, 17¾, 17½, 17, 17]"
46.5 [45.5, 45, 44.5, 43, 43] cm

14½ [16½, 18¼, 20½, 22½, 24¾]"
37 [42, 46.5, 52, 57, 63] cm

17¼ [19½, 21¼, 23½, 25½, 27¾]"
44 [49.5, 54, 59.5, 65, 70.5] cm

Rep the last 2 rows 0 (1, 0, 1, 1, 1) more time(s)—70 (76, 82, 88, 94, 100) sts rem.

Cont working even in St st until armhole meas 6½ (7, 7½, 8, 8½, 9)" (16.5 [18, 19, 20.5, 21.5, 23] cm), ending with a WS row.

Work in Gtr st for 1" (2.5 cm), ending with a WS row. BO all sts. Break yarn leaving a tail about 10" (25.5 cm) long for seaming.

Front

Work same as for back until armholes meas 3¼ (3½, 3¾, 4, 4¼, 4½)" (8.5 [9, 9.5, 10, 11, 11.5] cm), ending with a WS row—70 (76, 82, 88, 94, 100) sts.

Shape Upper Armholes

INC ROW: (RS) K2, M1L, work to last 2 sts, M1R, k2—2 sts inc'd.

Work even in St st for 3 rows, ending with a WS row.

Rep the last 4 rows 3 (3, 4, 5, 6, 6) more times, then work inc row once more—80 (86, 94, 102, 110, 116) sts.

Cont working even in St st until armholes meas 6½ (7, 7½, 8, 8½, 9)" (16.5 [18, 19, 20.5, 21.5, 23] cm), ending with a WS row.

Work in Gtr st for 1" (2.5 cm), ending with a WS row. BO all sts. Break yarn leaving a tail about 10" (25.5 cm) long for seaming.

Join Back and Front

Block pieces to measurements. Sew side seams.

Lay each front shoulder on top of each back shoulder for an overlap of 2½" (6.5 cm) at the side edge (see photo).

Using yarn tails from back and front, whipstitch along each overlap at the armhole edge.

Sleeve [make 2]

With dpn (dpn, 16" cir, 16" cir, 16" cir, 16" cir) and RS facing, beg at underarm seam, pick up and knit 76 (84, 96, 108, 120, 132) sts evenly around 1 armhole. Pm for beg of rnd and join to work in rnds.

SET-UP RND: K8 (7, 8, 9, 10, 11), pm, *k12 (14, 16, 18, 20, 22), pm; rep from * 4 more times, k8 (7, 8, 9, 10, 11).

INC RND 1: *Knit to 1 st before m, M1R, k1, sl m; rep from * 5 more times, knit to end—6 sts inc'd.

NEXT RND: Knit

INC RND 2: *Knit to m, sl m, k1, M1L; rep from * 5 more times, knit to end—6 sts inc'd.

NEXT RND: Knit.

Rep the last 4 rnds 13 (13, 14, 14, 15, 15) more times, changing to longer cir when sts no longer fit on dpn or shorter cir—244 (252, 276, 288, 312, 324) sts. Piece should meas 8¼ (8¼, 8¾, 8¾, 9¼, 9¼)" (21 [21, 22, 22, 23.5, 23.5] cm) from pick-up rnd.

Work in Gtr st for 1" (2.5 cm), ending with purl rnd. BO all sts kwise.

Work second sleeve same as the first.

Finishing

Weave in ends. Block again if desired.

Get Inspired

Built in 400 B.C. as a Greek shrine dedicated to Erichthonius, the child who was raised by Athena, the entire Erechtheion temple is crafted in white marble and black limestone friezes. Constructed on a slope housing four main compartments, it is the original home to the famous Porch of the Caryatids. Its six supporting columns are shaped as draped female figures, delicate ladies who seem to defy gravity by supporting a heavy entablature balanced only on their heads. These originals were removed from the temple and replaced by replicas, and you can find five of the six originals housed in the Acropolis Museum, with the other in the British Museum.

abbreviations

beg(s)	begin(s); beginning		**rep**	repeat(s); repeating
BO	bind off		**Rev St st**	reverse stockinette st
CC	contrasting color		**rnd(s)**	round(s)
cir	circular needles		**RS**	right side
cm	centimeter(s)		**s2kp**	slip 2 stitches knitwise, knit 1, pass the 2 slipped stitches under (2 stitch decrease)
cn	cable needle			
CO	cast on			
cont	continue(s); continuing		**sk2p**	slip 1, knit 2 stitches together, pass slipped stitch over (2 stitch decrease)
dec(s)	decrease(s); decreasing			
dpn	double-pointed needles		**sl**	slip
est	established		**sl st**	slip st (slip 1 stitch purlwise unless otherwise indicated)
foll	follow(s); following			
g	gram(s)		**ssk**	slip 2 stitches knitwise, one at a time, from the left needle to right needle, insert left needle tip through both front loops and knit together from this position (1 stitch decrease)
inc(s)	increase(s); increasing			
k	knit			
k1f&b	knit into the front and back of the same stitch			
			st(s)	stitch(es)
k1f&b&f	knit into the front, back, and front of the same stitch		**St st**	stockinette st
			tbl	through back loop
k2tog	knit 2 stitches together		**tog**	together
m	marker(s)		**WS**	wrong side
mm	millimeter(s)		**wyf**	with yarn in front
M1	make one (increase)		**wyb**	with yarn in back
MC	main color		**yd**	yard(s)
meas	measures		**yo**	yarnover
p	purl		*	repeat starting point
p2tog	purl 2 stitches together		**	repeat all instructions between asterisks
patt(s)	pattern(s)			
pm	place marker		()	alternate measurements and/or instructions
pwise	purlwise, as if to purl			
rem	remain(s); remaining		[]	work instructions as a group a specified number of times

techniques

Cast-Ons

Backward Loop Cast-On

*Loop working yarn and place it on needle backward so that it doesn't unwind. Repeat from *.

Cable Cast-On

If there are no stitches on the needle, make a slipknot of working yarn and place it on the needle, then use the knitted method to cast on one more stitch—two stitches on needle. Hold needle with working yarn in your left hand with the wrong side of the work facing you. *Insert right needle between the first two stitches on left needle *(Figure 1)*, wrap yarn around needle as if to knit, draw yarn through *(Figure 2)*, and place new loop on left needle *(Figure 3)* to form a new stitch. Repeat from * for the desired number of stitches, always working between the first two stitches on the left needle.

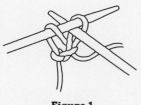

Figure 1

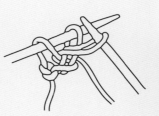

Figure 2

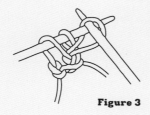

Figure 3

Provisional Cast-On

With waste yarn and crochet hook, make a loose crochet chain about four stitches more than you need to cast on. With knitting needle, working yarn, and beginning two stitches from end of chain, pick up and knit one stitch through the back loop of each crochet chain *(Figure 1)* for desired number of stitches. When you're ready to work in the opposite direction, pull out the crochet chain to expose live stitches *(Figure 2)*.

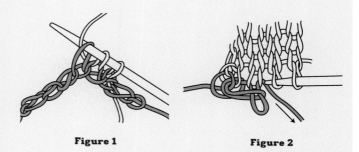

Figure 1   **Figure 2**

Judy's Magic Cast-On

This amazingly simple cast-on is named for its founder, Judy Becker. It wraps the yarn around two parallel needles in such a way as to mimic a row of stockinette stitch between the two needles.

Leaving a 10" (25.5 cm) tail, drape the yarn over one needle, then hold a second needle parallel to and below the first and on top of the yarn tail *(Figure 1)*.

Bring the tail to the back and the ball yarn to the front, then place the thumb and index finger of your left hand between the two strands so that the tail is over your index finger and the ball yarn is over your thumb *(Figure 2)*. This forms the first stitch on the top needle.

*Continue to hold the two needles parallel and loop the finger yarn over the lower needle by bringing the lower needle over the top of the finger yarn *(Figure 3)*, then bringing the finger yarn up from below the lower needle, over the top of this needle, then to the back between the two needles.

Point the needles downward, bring the bottom needle past the thumb yarn, then bring the thumb yarn to the front between the two needles and over the top needle *(Figure 4)*.

Repeat from * until you have the desired number of stitches on each needle *(Figure 5)*.

Remove both yarn ends from your left hand, rotate the needles like the hands of a clock so that the bottom needle is now on top and both strands of yarn are at the needle tip *(Figure 6)*.

Using a third needle, knit half of the stitches from the top needle *(Figure 7)*. There will now be the same number of stitches on two needles and twice that number of stitches on the bottom needle.

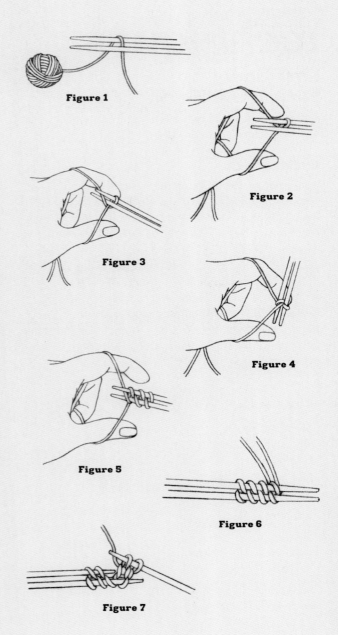

Figure 1

Figure 2

Figure 3

Figure 4

Figure 5

Figure 6

Figure 7

Knitted Cast-On

Make a slipknot of working yarn and place it on the left needle if there are no stitches already there. *Use the right needle to knit the first stitch (or slipknot) on left needle *(Figure 1)* and place new loop onto left needle to form a new stitch *(Figure 2)*. Repeat from * for the desired number of stitches, always working into the last stitch made.

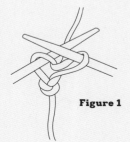

Figure 1

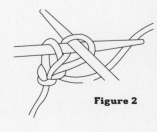

Figure 2

Long-Tail (Continental) Cast-On

Leaving a long tail (about ½" [1.3 cm] for each stitch to be cast on), make a slipknot and place on right needle. Place thumb and index finger of your left hand between the yarn ends so that working yarn is around your index finger and tail end is around your thumb and secure the yarn ends with your other fingers. Hold your palm upward, making a V of yarn *(Figure 1)*. *Bring needle up through loop on thumb *(Figure 2)*, catch first strand around index finger, and go back down through loop on thumb *(Figure 3)*. Drop loop off thumb and, placing thumb back in V configuration, tighten resulting stitch on needle *(Figure 4)*. Repeat from * for the desired number of stitches.

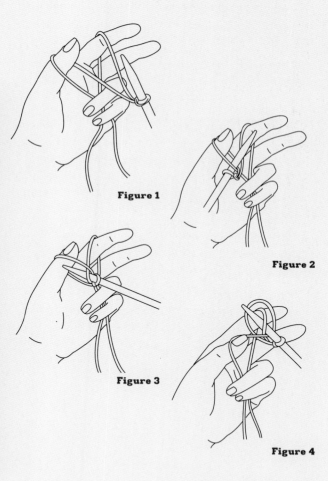

Figure 1

Figure 2

Figure 3

Figure 4

Turkish/Eastern Cast-On

This method is worked by first wrapping the yarn around two parallel needles, then using a third needle to knit the loops on each of the two needles. The loops on one needle are the foundation for the instep, and the loops on the other needle are the foundation for the sole.

Hold two double-pointed needles parallel to each other. Leaving a 4" (10 cm) tail hanging to the front between the two needles, wrap the yarn around both needles from back to front half the number of times as desired stitches (four wraps shown here for eight stitches total), then bring the yarn forward between the needles *(Figure 1)*.

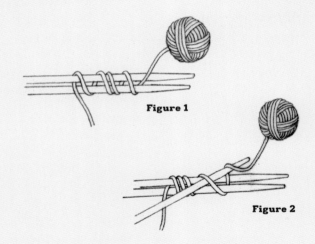

Figure 1

Use a third needle to knit across the loops on the top needle, keeping the third needle on top of both the other needles when knitting the first stitch *(Figure 2)*.

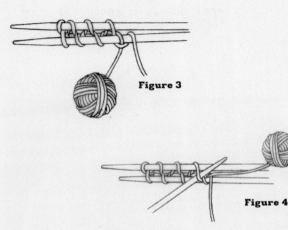

Figure 2

With the right side facing, rotate the two cast-on needles like the hands of a clock so that the bottom needle is on the top *(Figure 3)*.

Knit across the loops on the new top needle *(Figure 4)*.

Rotate the needles again and use a third needle to knit the first two stitches of the new top needle. There will now be two stitches each on two needles and four stitches on another needle *(Figure 5)*.

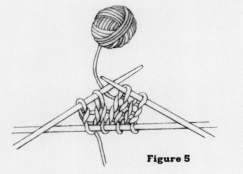

Figure 3

Figure 4

Figure 5

Bind-Offs

Jeny's Surprisingly Stretchy Bind-Off

This aptly named bind-off is the brainchild of Jeny Staiman. The elasticity comes from a yarnover "collar" that is worked in conjunction with each stitch. When viewed straight on, the bind-off edge of the ribbing will have a hinged appearance at each transition between knit and purl stitches.

To Collar a Knit Stitch: Bring working yarn from back to front over needle in the opposite direction of a normal yarnover *(Figure 1)*, knit the next stitch, then lift the yarnover over the top of the knitted stitch and off the needle *(Figure 2)*.

To Collar a Purl Stitch: Bring working yarn from front to back over needle as for a normal yarnover *(Figure 3)*, purl the next stitch, then lift the yarnover over the top of the purled stitch and off the needle *(Figure 4)*.

To begin, collar each of the first two stitches to match their knit or purl nature. Then pass the first collared stitch over the second and off the right needle—one stitch is bound off.

*Collar the next stitch according to its nature *(Figure 5)*, then pass the previous stitch over the collared stitch and off the needle *(Figure 6)*.

Repeat from * until one stitch remains on the right needle. Cut the yarn, leaving a 6" (15 cm) tail, then pull on the loop of the last stitch until the tail comes free.

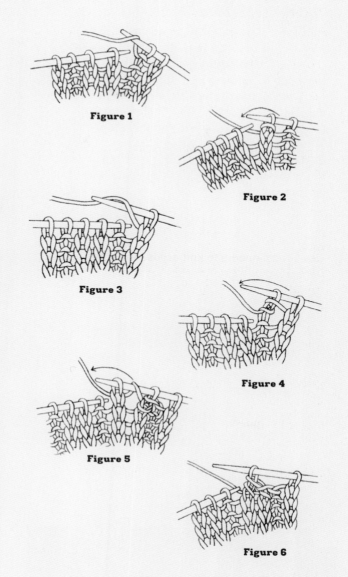

Figure 1

Figure 2

Figure 3

Figure 4

Figure 5

Figure 6

Three-Needle Bind-Off

Place the stitches to be joined onto two separate needles and hold the needles parallel so that the two sides of knitting face together. Insert a third needle into the first stitch on each of two needles *(Figure 1)* and knit them together as one stitch *(Figure 2)*, *knit the next stitch on each needle the same way, then use the left needle tip to lift the first stitch over the second and off the needle *(Figure 3)*. Repeat from * until no stitches remain on first two needles. Cut yarn and pull tail through last stitch to secure.

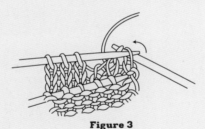

Figure 1

Figure 2

Figure 3

Decreases

Knit 2 Together [k2tog]

Knit two stitches together as if they were a single stitch.

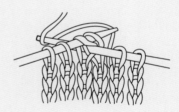

Purl 2 Together [p2tog]

Purl two stitches together as if they were a single stitch.

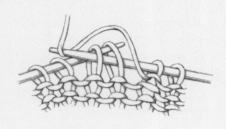

Slip, Slip, Knit [ssk]

Slip two stitches individually knitwise *(Figure 1)*, insert left needle tip into the front of these two slipped stitches, and use the right needle to knit them together through their back loops *(Figure 2)*.

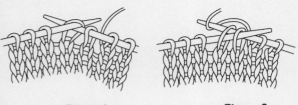

Figure 1   **Figure 2**

Slip, Slip, Purl (ssp)

This type of decrease slants to the left. Holding yarn in front, slip two stitches individually knitwise **(Figure 1)**, then slip these two stitches back onto left needle (they will be twisted on the needle) and purl them together through their back loops **(Figure 2)**.

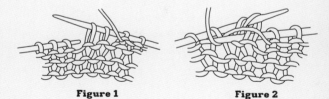

Figure 1   Figure 2

Increases

Lifted Increase (LI)

This type of increase is nearly invisible in the knitting. It can be worked to slant to the right or to the left, which can be used as a design element along raglan shaping. You can separate the increases by the desired number of stitches to form a prominent ridge.

For circular-yoke shaping, use the slant of your choice.

Right Slant (RLI): Knit into the back of the stitch (in the "purl bump") in the row directly below the first stitch on the left needle **(Figure 1)**, then knit the stitch on the needle **(Figure 2)** and slip the original stitch off the needle.

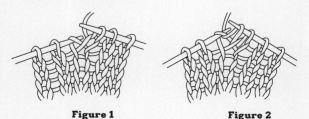

Figure 1   Figure 2

Left Slant (LLI): Knit the first stitch on the left needle, insert left needle tip into the back of the stitch (in the "purl bump") below the stitch just knitted **(Figure 1)**, then knit this stitch **(Figure 2)**.

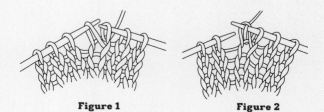

Figure 1   Figure 2

Raised Make-One Increase [M1]

This type of increase is characterized by the tiny twisted stitch that forms at the base of the increase. Like the lifted method, it can slant to the right or the left, and you can separate the increases by the desired number of stitches to form a prominent ridge.

Right Slant (M1R): Use the left needle tip to lift the strand between the needle tips from back to front **(Figure 1)**, then knit the lifted loop through the front to twist it **(Figure 2)**.

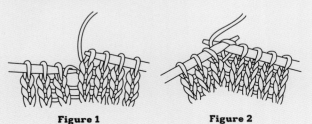

Figure 1   **Figure 2**

Left Slant (M1L): Use the left needle tip to lift the strand between the needle tips from front to back **(Figure 1)**, then knit the lifted loop through the back to twist it **(Figure 2)**.

You can work these increases purlwise (M1P) by purling the lifted strand instead of knitting it.

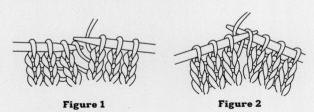

Figure 1   **Figure 2**

Short Rows
Knit Side

Work to turning point, slip next stitch purlwise **(Figure 1)**, bring the yarn to the front, then slip the same stitch back to the left needle **(Figure 2)**, turn the work around and bring the yarn in position for the next stitch—one stitch has been wrapped and the yarn is correctly positioned to work the next stitch. When you come to a wrapped stitch on a subsequent row, hide the wrap by working it together with the wrapped stitch as follows: Insert right needle tip under the wrap (from the front if wrapped stitch is a knit stitch; from the back if wrapped stitch is a purl stitch; **Figure 3**), then into the stitch on the needle, and work the stitch and its wrap together as a single stitch.

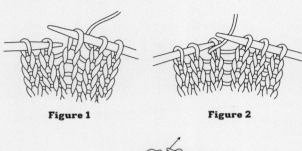

Figure 1   **Figure 2**

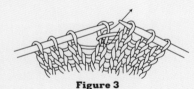

Figure 3

Purl Side

Work to the turning point, slip the next stitch purlwise to the right needle, bring the yarn to the back of the work *(Figure 1)*, return the slipped stitch to the left needle, bring the yarn to the front between the needles *(Figure 2)*, and turn the work so that the knit side is facing—one stitch has been wrapped and the yarn is correctly positioned to knit the next stitch. To hide the wrap on a subsequent purl row, work to the wrapped stitch, use the tip of the right needle to pick up the wrap from the back, place it on the left needle *(Figure 3)*, then purl it together with the wrapped stitch.

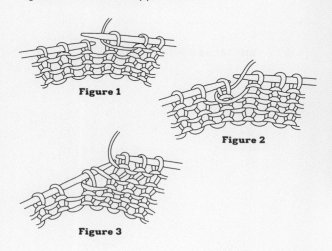

Figure 1

Figure 2

Figure 3

Wrap & Turn [w&t]

Work to turn point, slip next stitch purlwise to right needle *(Figure 1)*. Bring yarn to front *(Figure 2)*. Slip same stitch back to left needle *(Figure 3)*. Turn work and bring yarn in position for next stitch, wrapping the stitch as you do so.

Note: *Hide wraps in a knit stitch when right side of piece is worked in a knit stitch. Leave wrap if the purl stitch shows on right side.*

Hide wraps as follows:

Knit stitch: On right side, work to just before wrapped stitch. Insert right needle from front, under the wrap from bottom up, and then into wrapped stitch as usual. Knit them together, making sure new stitch comes out under wrap.

Purl stitch: On wrong side, work to just before wrapped stitch. Insert right needle from back, under wrap from bottom up, and put on left needle. Purl them together.

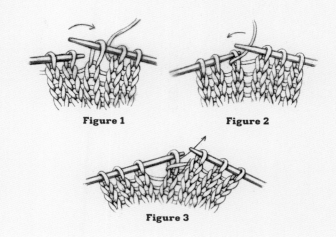

Figure 1   **Figure 2**

Figure 3

Kitchener Stitch

Arrange stitches on two needles so that there is the same number of stitches on each needle. Hold the needles parallel to each other with wrong sides of the knitting together. Allowing about ½" (1.3 cm) per stitch to be grafted, thread matching yarn on a tapestry needle. Work from right to left as follows:

STEP 1. Bring tapestry needle through the first stitch on the front needle as if to purl and leave the stitch on the needle *(Figure 1)*.

STEP 2. Bring tapestry needle through the first stitch on the back needle as if to knit and leave that stitch on the needle *(Figure 2)*.

STEP 3. Bring tapestry needle through the first front stitch as if to knit and slip this stitch off the needle, then bring tapestry needle through the next front stitch as if to purl and leave this stitch on the needle *(Figure 3)*.

STEP 4. Bring tapestry needle through the first back stitch as if to purl and slip this stitch off the needle, then bring tapestry needle through the next back stitch as if to knit and leave this stitch on the needle *(Figure 4)*.

Repeat Steps 3 and 4 until one stitch remains on each needle, adjusting the tension to match the rest of the knitting as you go. To finish, bring tapestry needle through the front stitch as if to knit and slip this stitch off the needle, then bring tapestry needle through the back stitch as if to purl and slip this stitch off the needle.

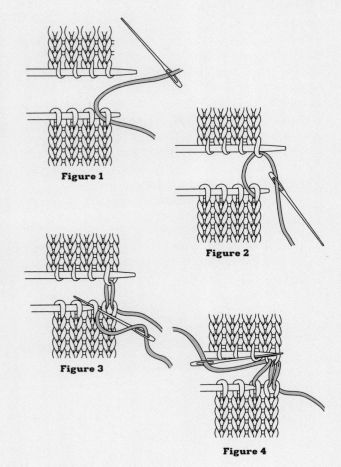

Figure 1

Figure 2

Figure 3

Figure 4

sources for yarns

BE SWEET
1315 Bridgeway
Sausalito, CA 94965
(415) 331-9676
besweetproducts.com

BERROCO
1 Tupperware Dr., Ste. 4,
North Smithfield, RI 02896
(401) 769-1212
berroco.com

BLUE MOON FIBER ARTS
56587 Mollenhour Rd.
Scappoose, OR 97056
(866) 802-9687
bluemoonfiberarts.com

BROOKLYNTWEED
brooklyntweed.net

CASCADE YARNS
PO Box 58158
Seattle, WA 98138
cascadeyarns.com

CLASSIC ELITE YARNS
16 Esquire Rd., Unit 2
North Billerica, MA 01862
(800) 343-0308
classiceliteyarns.com

DREAM IN COLOR
dreamincoloryarn.com

THE FIBRE COMPANY
2000 Manor Rd.
Conshohocken, PA 19428
(484) 368-3666
thefibreco.com

HAZEL KNITS
hazelknits.com

**IMPERIAL STOCK
RANCH YARN**
92462 Hinton Rd.
Maupin, OR 97037
(541) 395-2507
imperialyarn.com

ISAGER
218 Galisteo St.
Santa Fe, NM 87501
(505) 982-8356
knitisager.com

LORNA'S LACES
4229 North Honore St.
Chicago, IL 60613
(773) 935-3803
lornaslaces.net

LOUET NORTH AMERICA
3425 Hands Rd.
Prescott, ON
Canada K0E 1T0
(800) 897-6444
louet.com

**MISSBABS HAND-DYED
YARNS & FIBERS**
P.O. Box 78
Mountain City, TN 37683
(423) 727-0670
missbabs.com

**NEIGHBORHOOD FIBER
COMPANY**
neighborhoodfiberco.com

PEACE FLEECE
475 Porterfield Rd.
Porter, ME 04068
peacefleece.com

QUINCE & CO.
quinceandco.com

ROWAN YARNS
Green Lane Mill
Holmfirth, West Yorkshire
England HD9 2DX
+44 (0)1484 681881
knitrowan.com

USA: Westminster Fibers
165 Ledge St.
Nashua, NH 03060
(800) 445-9276
westminsterfibers.com

SWEETGEORGIA
110-408 East Kent Ave.
Vancouver, BC
Canada V5X 2X7
(604) 569-6811
sweetgeorgiayarns.com

TANIS FIBER ARTS
tanisfiberarts.com

WOOLMEISE
Rohrspatz & Wollmeise
Schulstraße 10
85276 Pfaffenhofen
wollmeise-yarnshop.de

about the designers

Amy Christoffers lives in Vermont and can be found online at savoryknitting.com.

Having learned to knit at her mother's knee, **Olga Buraya-Kefelian's** love of design began at a very young age. Seeking inspiration from industrial and architectural sources, she strives to translate those experiences through her work with knitwear. Author of *Ori Ami Knits: Fiber Geometry*, Olga resides in Virginia, where she designs her own line of garments and accessories. See more from her at olgajazzy.com.

Jane Dupuis loves architecture and mittens. She lives with her husband and avian companion, Pookie, in Windsor, Ontario, where she playfully combines the two.

Grace Anna Farrow learned to knit in the third grade on pick-up sticks. Nowadays she knits on ordinary knitting needles at astitchtowear.com.

Tanis Gray is the former yarn editor for Soho Publishing and the author of *Knit Local* (Sixth & Spring, 2011), *Capitol Knits* (self-published, 2011), and this book. With more than three hundred published knitting designs in books and magazines worldwide, Tanis thinks knitting is the best thing in the world. Currently residing outside of Washington, D.C. with her mechanical engineer husband, toddler son, and lazy pug, she's furiously working on her next project. Check out more of her work and writings at tanisknits.com.

After many years practicing as a veterinarian, **Angela Hahn** decided to practice knitwear design instead. She and her family divide their time between Cape Cod, Massachusetts, and Como, Italy. Texture and lace worked in unexpected directions, unusual methods of shaping, and decreases and increases worked into stitch patterns—these are some of the elements that Angela enjoys including in her designs. Find more of her patterns on her website, knititude.com.

Marjan Hammink is a knitter/designer who lives in the Netherlands with her husband and three sons. She's passionate about designing knitwear that shows individuality.

Having learned to knit as a child, **Glenna Harris** became a true knitter several years ago while studying for her Ph.D., as a form of stress relief and distraction. She finished the Ph.D. and kept on knitting anyway. Having since added knitting design and teaching to her repertoire, Glenna enjoys encouraging knitters to continue learning, and produces knitting patterns for publication, self-publication, and in collaboration with independent yarn dyers. She has a yarn stash with a life of its own and is never without a project no matter the location. Her design philosophy is guided by a desire to knit things that are comfortable and wearable, but more importantly, to continue challenging herself with interesting techniques and beautiful results, through cables, colorwork, and more. Glenna believes in knitting fearlessly and often. She blogs twice weekly at crazyknittinglady.wordpress.com.

Kirsten Kapur has been knitting, sewing, and creating for as long as she can remember. She worked for many years as a fashion and then textile designer in New York City. Designing knitting patterns allows her the opportunity to combine her love of garment construction and surface design. She has had patterns published in several books and magazines including *Knitty*, *Knit Simple*, *Knitscene*, *The Joy of Sox*, *Brave New Knits*, *Knitting It Old School*, *Knit Local*, *My Grandmother's Knitting*, *Craft Activism*, and *Weekend Hats*. You will find her blogging about her knitting on throughtheloops.typepad.com, where she also self-publishes her designs.

Tanis Lavallée is an artist and dyer living in Montreal, Quebec. She runs her hand-dyed yarn company, Tanis Fiber Arts, with her husband, Chris. Tanis loves nothing more than knitting warm woolies for her loved ones, including her four-year-old whippet, Stella, who has an extensive wardrobe of handknit sweaters. Tanis's favorite color is blue.

Maria Leigh is a fashion designer who relocated from Seoul, Korea, to Athens, Ontario. She's embracing the culture and language of her new home. Her first English pattern was written in 2008, and she is publishing her designs in major magazines. Read her blog at amigurumikr.com.

Cecily Glowik MacDonald lives in beautiful Portland, Maine, with her husband, Ethan. She spends her days (and nights!) knitting, designing, and trying to keep track of it all on her blog, cecilyam.wordpress.com.

Mari Muinonen is a knitter and teacher in Finland. Besides knitting and nowadays spinning, she loves her family, good coffee, and techno gadgets. You can read more about Mari's crafts and designs on her blog, Madebymyself, at madebymyself.blogspot.fi.

Katharina Nopp graduated with a degree in media design in 2004 and started studying German literature and cultural studies in Vienna. Since working as a graphic designer, she's been focusing on the interrelation of arts and literature and started knitting to stop thinking and reading for a while. In 2010 Katharina and her friend started their own hand-dyed yarn brand, umschlagWolle, which can be found at umschlagplatz.at.

Best-selling author **Kristin Omdahl** designs knit and crochet garments and patterns under her label, KRISTIN, and website, styledbykristin.com. She appears on *Knitting Daily TV* and teaches knitting and crochet in her DVD workshops. She is the author of *Wrapped in Crochet*, *Crochet So Fine*, *A Knitting Wrapsody*, *Seamless Crochet*, and *The Finer Edge.* She lives in Florida.

Cirilia Rose lives in the Pacific Northwest and is creative director for Skacel Collection Inc. She spends her days tangled up in yarn and her evenings making messes in the kitchen. She loves the ornate, idiosyncratic architecture of Providence and Chicago, and her favorite architect is Friedensreich Hundertwasser. You can follow her fiber exploits at skacelfiberstudio.com and bricoleurknits.com.

Suvi Simola has knit on and off since childhood. She loves designs with clever details to pique knitters' interest and put a happy smile on their faces. She blogs about her knitting at 50villapeikkoa.blogspot.com.

Åsa Söderman is the woman behind Åsa Tricosa. She knits with abandon in many parts of the world. Not because she's in such high demand, but because she happens to move a lot—on the fringes of academia. When she isn't solving knitting riddles or working out unorthodox methods, she is thinking about what to make next while learning German. She will happily knit the wrong way if that gets her to the other end of a sideways shawl. Åsa grew up in Sweden and lived in the United States and then England for many years. She now lives in Germany, mostly, and has been knitting since about age three. You can find her on asatricosa.com.

Veera Välimäki is a Finnish designer living in a small house in Southern Finland. Her knitting designs have been published in *Knitscene*, *Madelinetosh*, and online at rainknitwear.com. She's interested in modern sweater designs worked seamlessly and is eager to teach both of her sons to knit.

Ann Weaver has been designing handknits since 2007 while working a growing string of seemingly unrelated jobs. Her work has been featured in *Knitty*, *Interweave Knits*, *Knitscene*, *Knit Now*, and many books. She also has self-published several collections of original patterns, including two inspired by *Moby-Dick*: *White Whale Vol. I* (October 2011) and *White Whale Vol. II* (October 2012). Her current projects include a series of patterns based on container ships and ship breaking. She currently lives in Baltimore, where she works as an editorial project manager and copyeditor.

acknowledgments

For Mom and Dad, who helped lay a strong foundation and construct the framework of my life, and provided me with the materials I needed to build my dream.

I am honored to be in the company of such talented and clever knitters, without whom this book simply would not have been possible. You rose to the challenge, and together we inspired each other.

To Erica Smith, my fearless editor and amazing friend, my deepest gratitude. You took my blueprints and notes, polished them up, and helped me build something grand.

To Kristen TenDyke, a heartfelt thanks for your tech editing genius.

Thank you to editorial director Allison Korleski for taking my idea and making it a reality.

Many thanks to associate art director Julia Boyles, photographer Joe Hancock, and his team for their talent.

index

looking for more ideas to knit?
FIND FRESH INSPIRATION WITH THESE INTERWEAVE RESOURCES

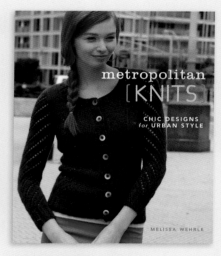